Cut & Collage

A Treasury of Bizarre & Beautiful Images for Collage & Mixed Media Artists

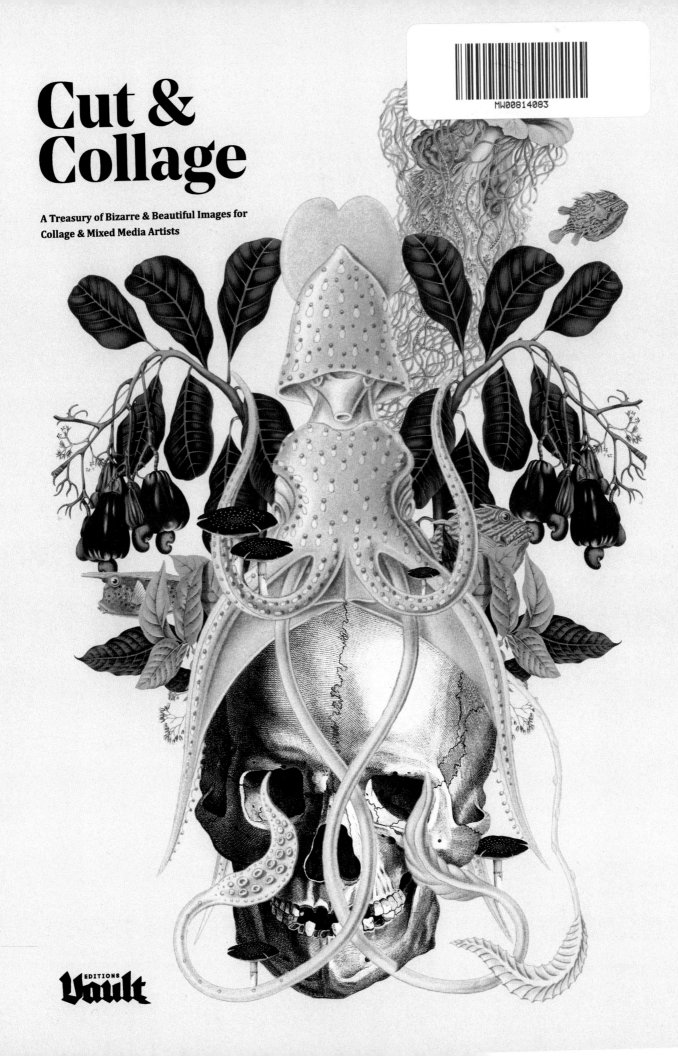

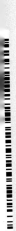

EDITIONS Vault

Introduction

This publication was created and curated for the practical use of collage and mixed-media artists. Featured within the pages of this volume are stunning full-colour anatomical illustrations, incredibly rendered botanical and sea life artwork including octopi, squid, pufferfish, eels and more. Also featured are a compelling collection of birds, snakes, surgical equipment, skulls, circus freaks, tattooed men, insects, animals and oddities.

Features:

We understand that mistakes happen when working with paper crafts, which is why we have included a unique download link that will provide you with access to a print-ready PDF of all artwork featured. Reuse your favourite images as many times as you like without having to scan or purchase the publication again. Accessing the

PDF will allow you to scale the size of the images so that the pieces of your collage fit together perfectly.

When accessing your downloadable PDF, you will also get the Vault Editions Skulls and Anatomy sample pack completely free.

About the author:

This book was curated and authored by the creative director of Vault Editions, Kale James. Kale has published over 12 acclaimed books within the art design space and has worked with brands including Nike, Samsung, Adidas and Rolling Stone. Kale's artwork is published in numerous titles including No Cure, Semi-Permanent, Vogue and more.

Whether you're an advanced collage artist or a first-timer looking to explore creative outlets, this book will provide you with the necessary means to make artwork that will impress both your clients and peers.

Gain access to your files and start creating bizarre and beautiful collages today.

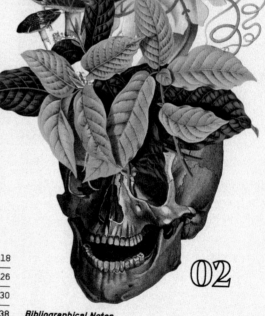

Download Your PDF

Table of Contents

Downloading your files is simple. To access the download page, please go to the following url and enter your unique password. Please then follow the prompts to download your files.

Download Page:

www.vaulteditions.com/caa

Unique Password:

caa0948272dg

For technical assistance, please contact:

info@vaulteditions.com

Bibliographical Notes

This is a new work by Avenue House Press PTY LTD.

Copyright

Copyright ©Avenue House Press Pty Ltd 2020.

ISBN: 978-1-925968-30-9

Recommended Materials

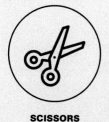
SCISSORS

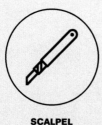
SCALPEL

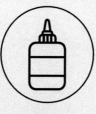
GLUE

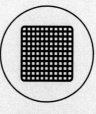
CUTTING MAT

HEAVY WEIGHT CARD

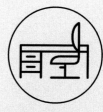
SAFE WORKSPACE

Collage is arguably one of the most experimental forms of visual art, and there are certainly no hard and fast rules on best practices. However, some essential tools and materials that will assist you in achieving the best results and will ensure the durability of your artwork.

Scissors:

We recommend a sharp pair of craft scissors to ensure that you avoid tearing the paper. It will also allow you to gain greater detail in every cut and will prevent micro—tearing and fraying edges which may occur with a lesser quality product.

Glue:

The glue you are using mustn't contain too much moisture. An excess of moisture will lead to cockling of the paper which can leave an undesirable lumpy finish. It can also cause bleeding of the ink. We recommend either a high—quality glue stick for beginners, and spray adhesive for the more advanced.

Scalpel:

For extracting detailed elements from an image, we recommend using a sharp scalpel for best results. Ensure that you regularly change your blade to avoid fraying edge and micro—tears.

Cutting Mat:

A cutting mat is essential for anyone working with a scalpel. They're relatively inexpensive and can be purchased from any good arts and crafts store. They are a worthy investment to save your desk or table from unwanted cut marks.

Substrates:

What surface should I apply my collage to? Again, there are no rules here, but we would recommend a heavy card of 350gsm or higher. If you intend to sell or gift your artwork, also consider using a paper size that will be compatible with standard frame sizes.

Workspace:

As you will be working with sharp tools, and generally making a bit of a mess, we recommend that you have an appropriate workspace with plenty of room to move. Ensure that your elbows are elevated above the table so that you have greater control of your movements when cutting to avoid slipping and any unwanted accidents. If you are working for long periods, consider investing in an ergonomic chair or standing desk to protect your back. These can be purchased from all good office supply stores. Many online reatilers will also have these available.

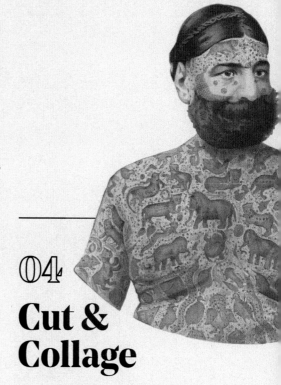

Cut & Collage

There are endless combinations and surprising juxtapositions to be discovered throughout the process of creating collages. The are no limits and no rules, so get cutting and be sure to share your results with us on Instagram @vault_editions so that we can share them with our community.

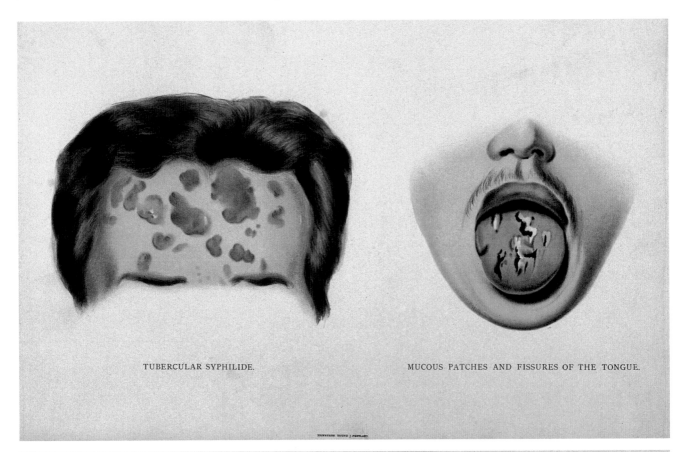

TUBERCULAR SYPHILIDE.

MUCOUS PATCHES AND FISSURES OF THE TONGUE.

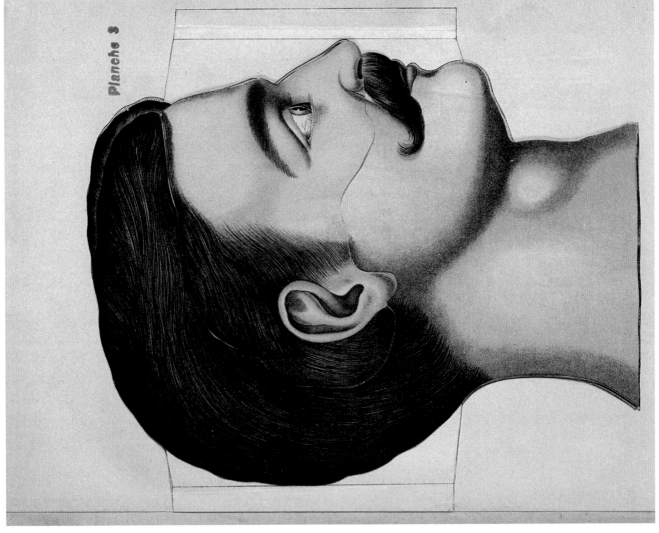

Pl. 1.

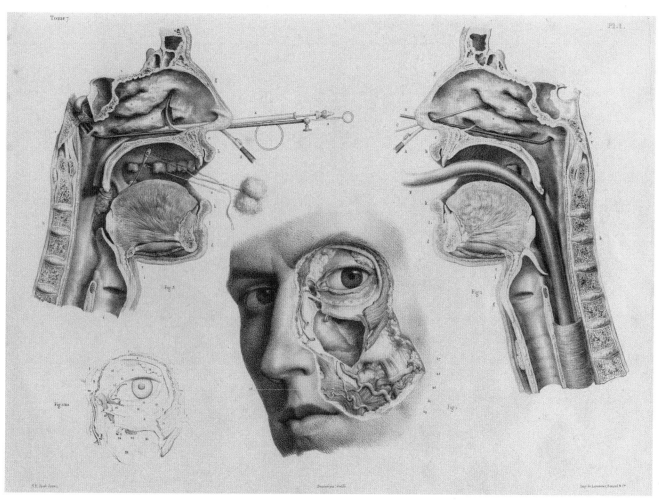

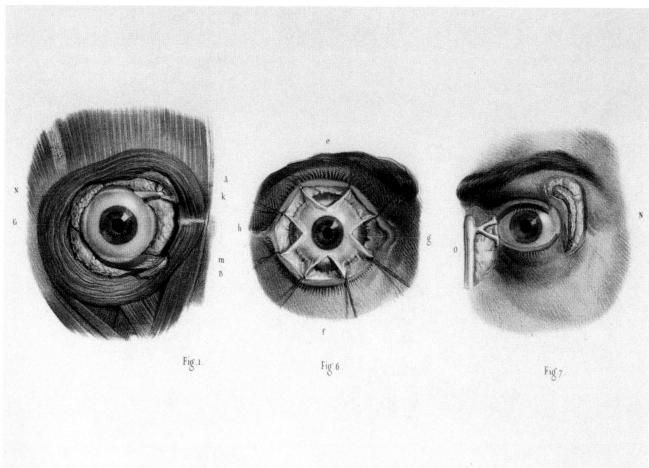

Fig. 1.   Fig. 6.   Fig. 7

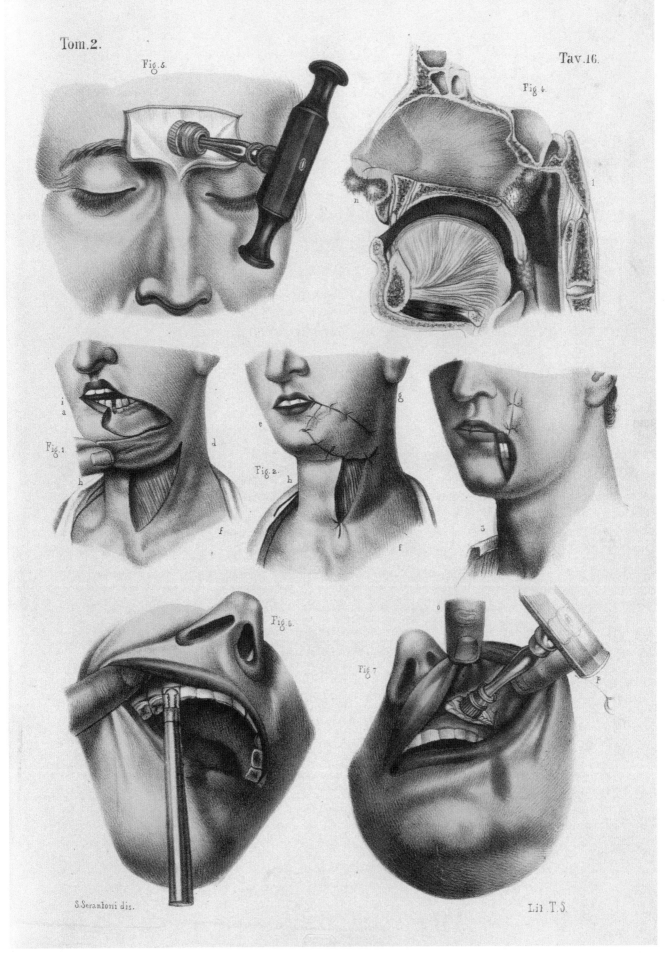

Tom.2.

Fig.5.

Tav.16.

Fig.4.

Fig.1.

Fig.2.

Fig.6.

Fig.7.

S.Seranloni dis.

Lit.T.S.

Pl.94.

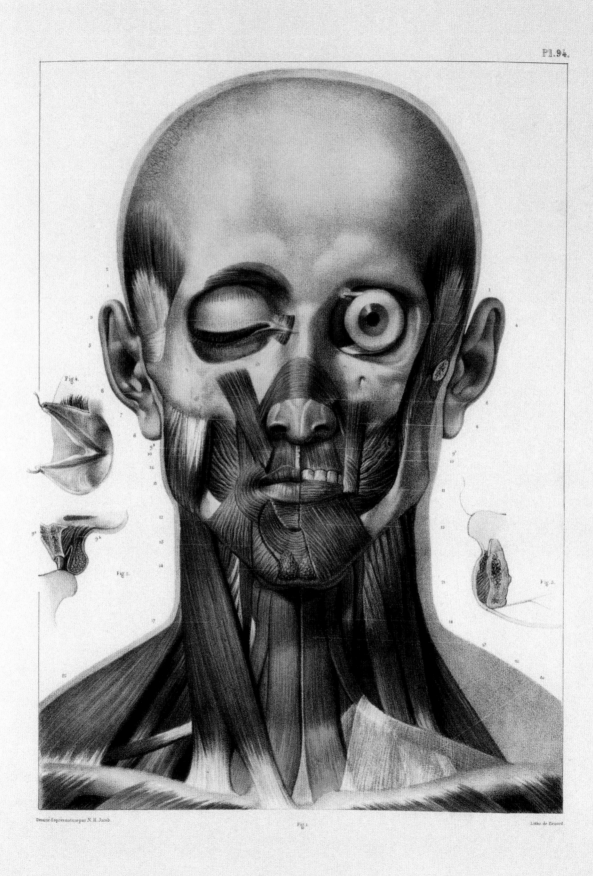

Dessiné d'après nature par N.H. Jacob.

Fig.1.

Litho. de Bequet.

PLATE XX.

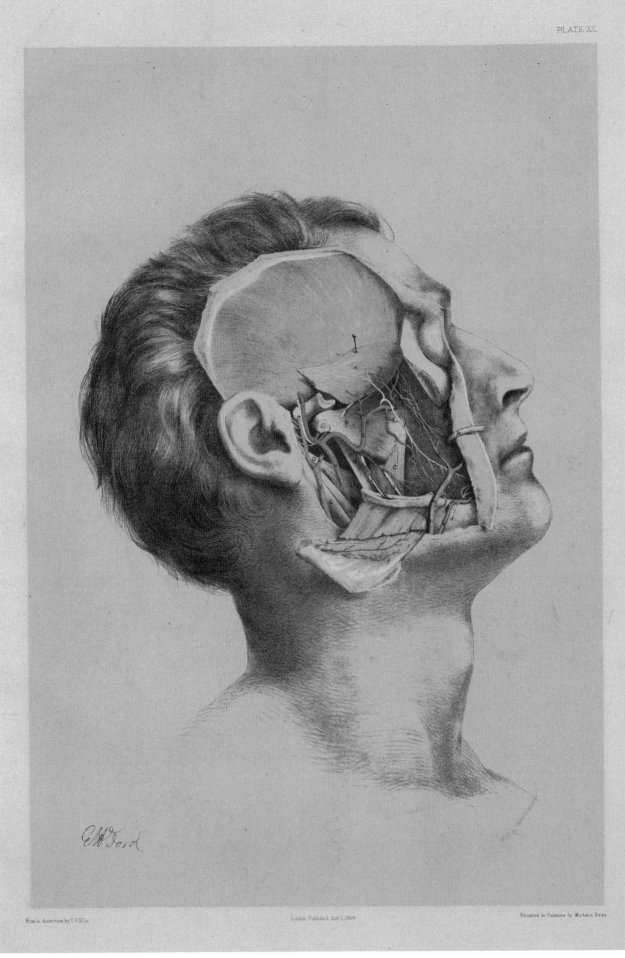

From a dissection by C.V.Ellis

London. Published July 1, 1864

Printed in Colours by Mintern Bros

PLATE XX.

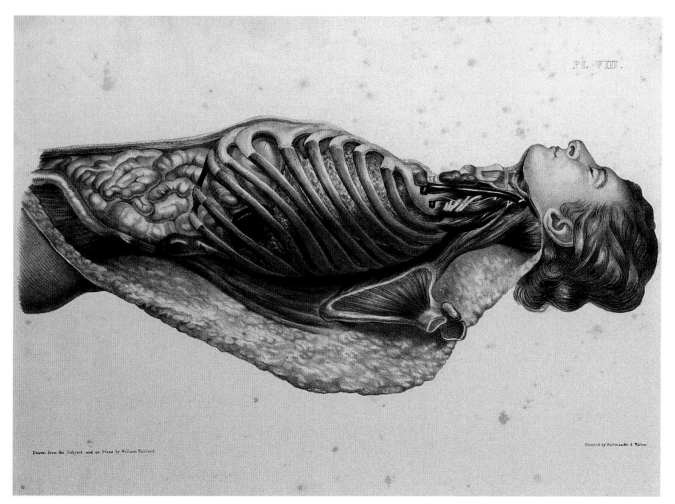

PL. VIII.

Drawn from the Subject and on Stone by William Fairland

Printed by Hullmandel & Walton

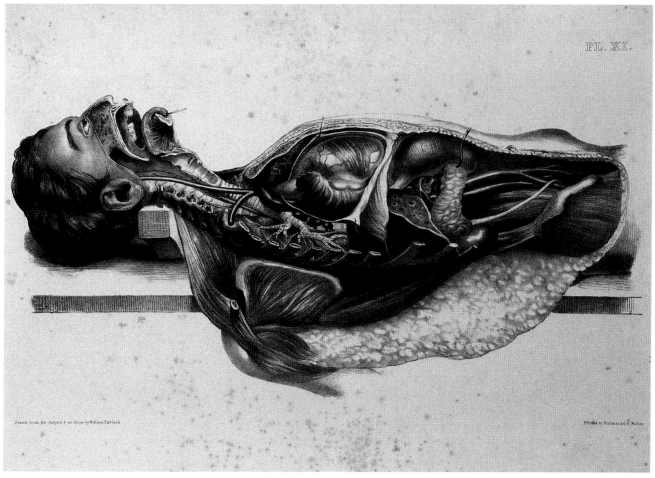

PL. XI.

Drawn from the Subject & on Stone by William Fairland

Printed by Hullmandel del E Walton

PL. VI.

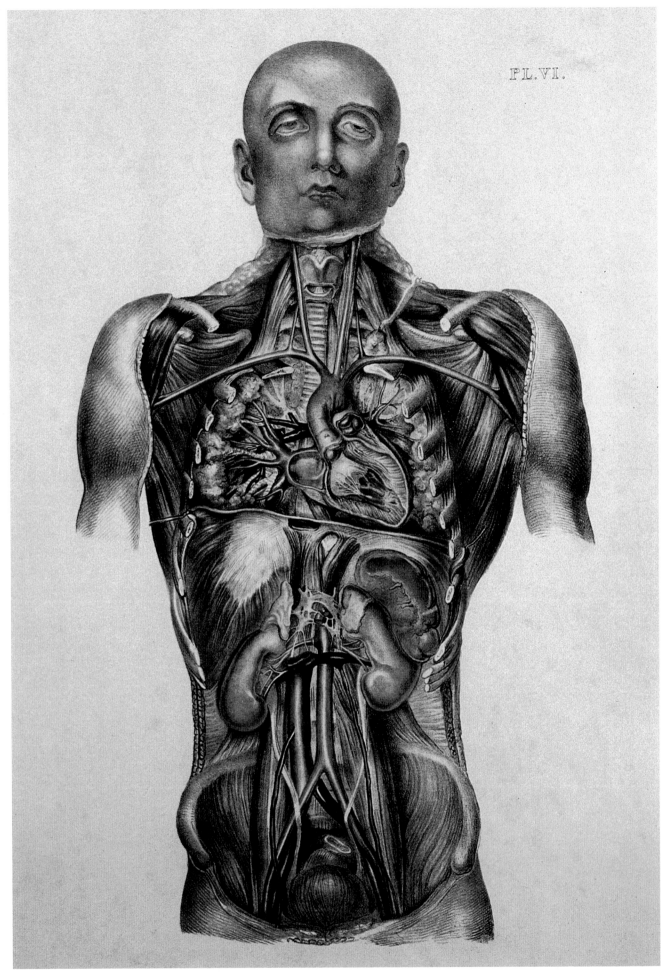

PL. V.

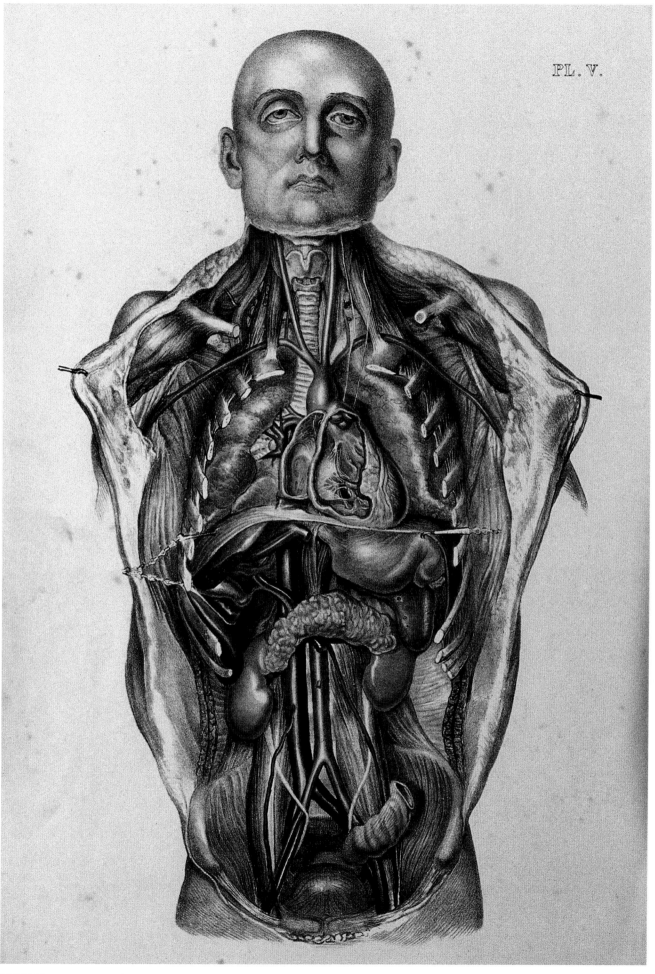

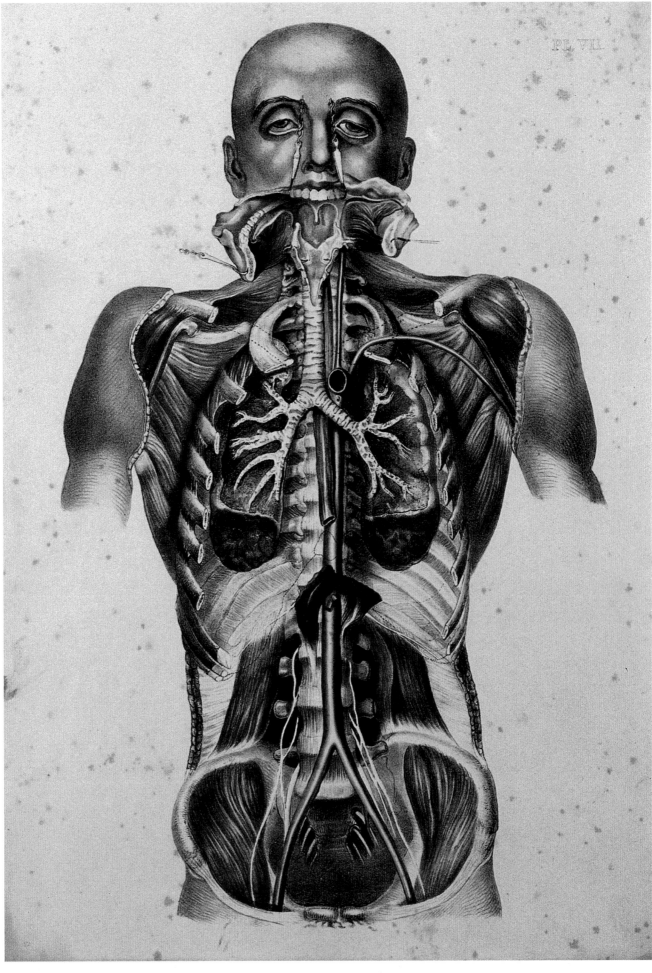

CUT & COLLAGE

PL. III.

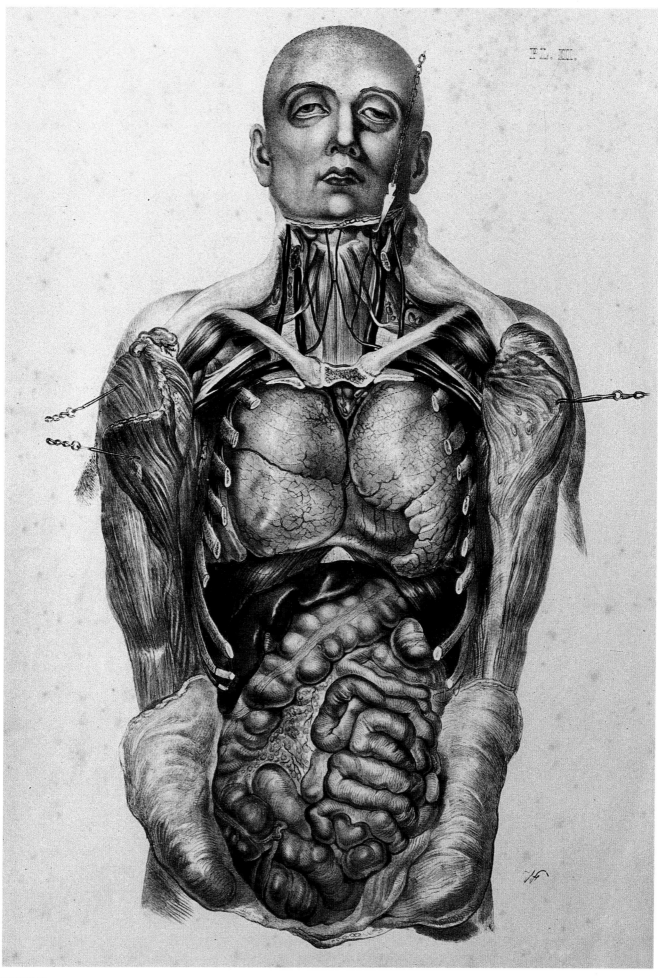

CUT & COLLAGE

PL. II.

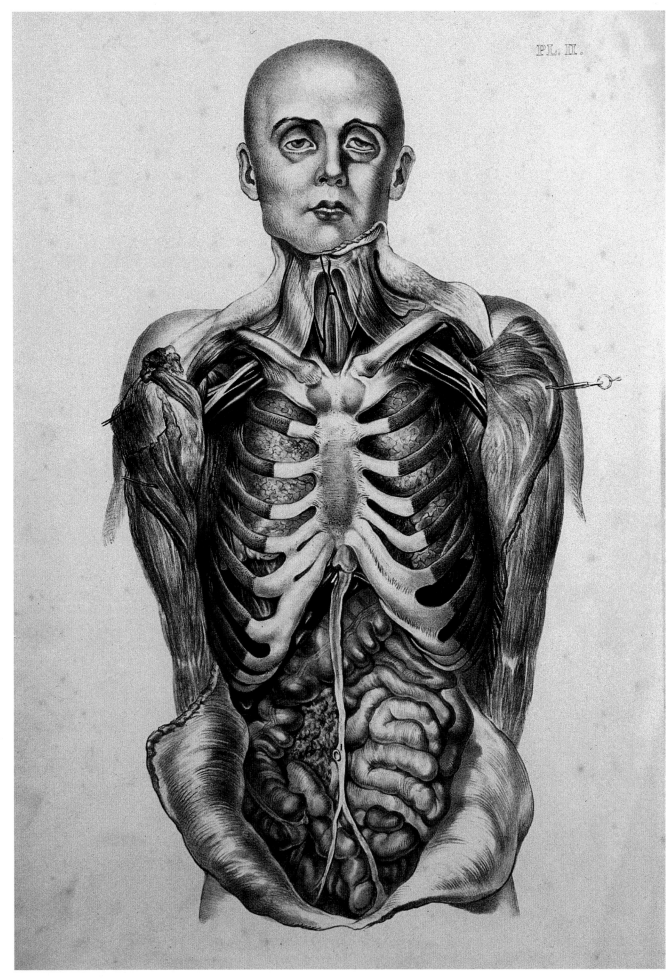

PL. IV.

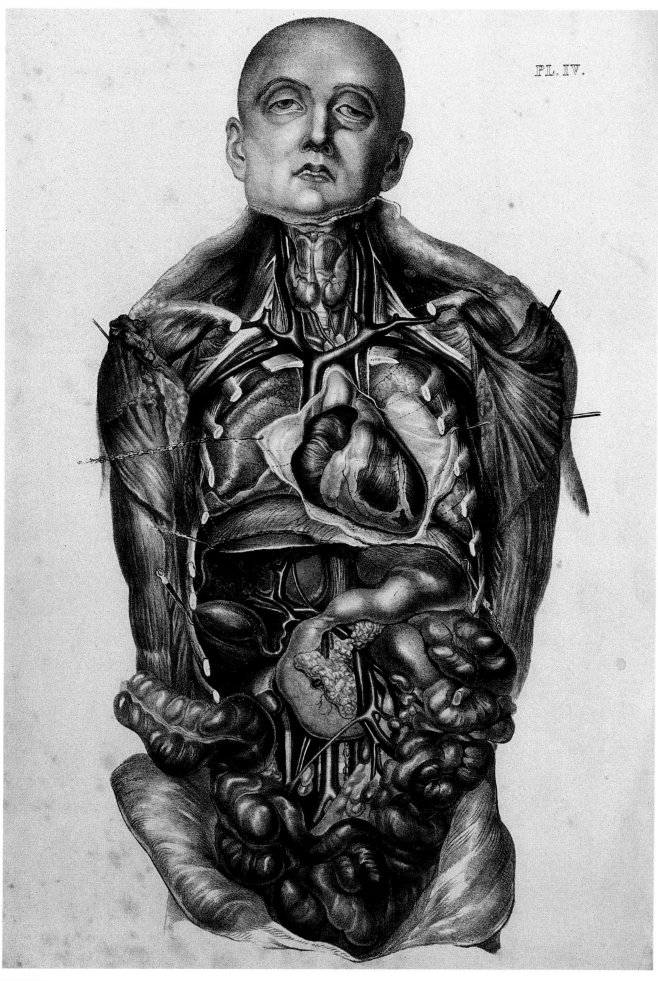

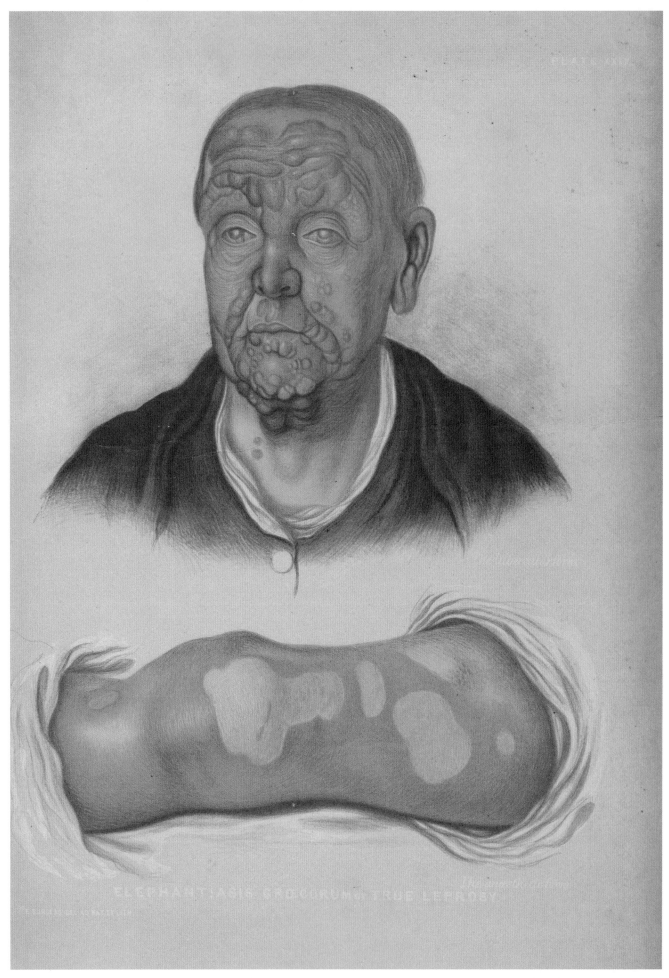

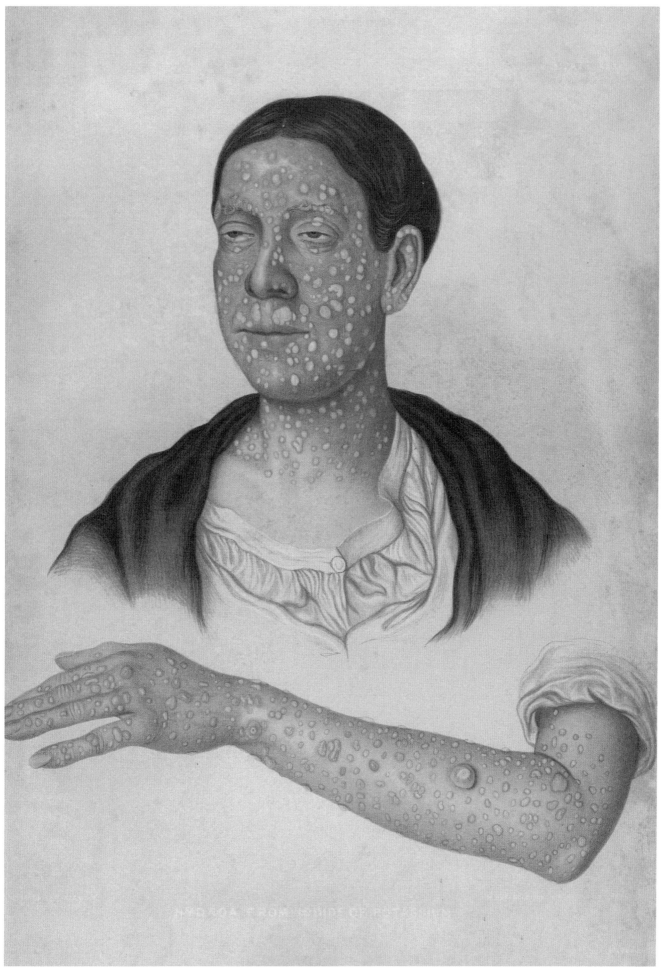

PLATE XLIII.

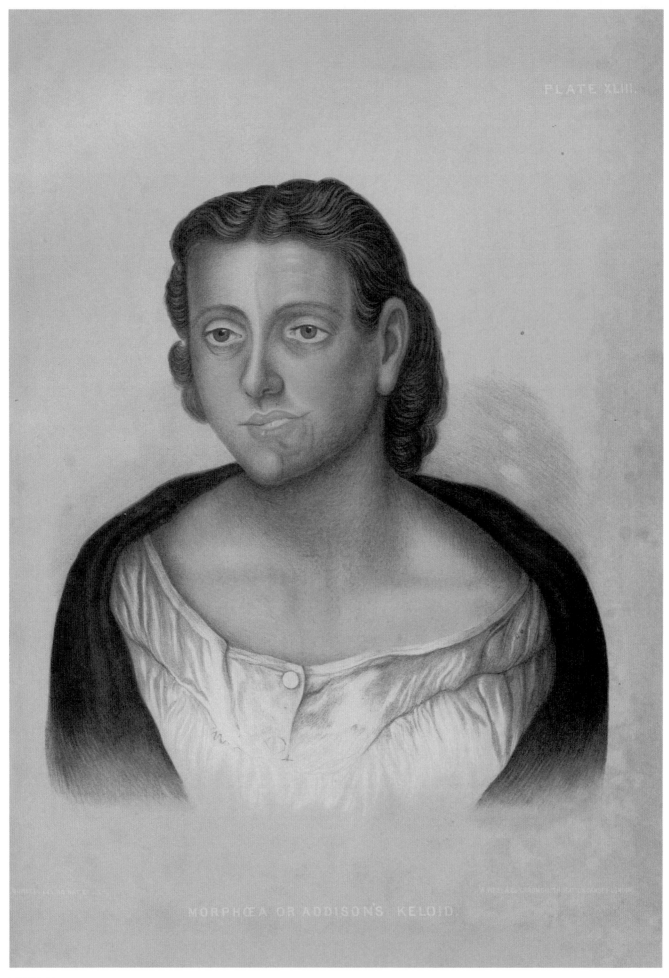

MORPHŒA OR ADDISON'S KELOID.

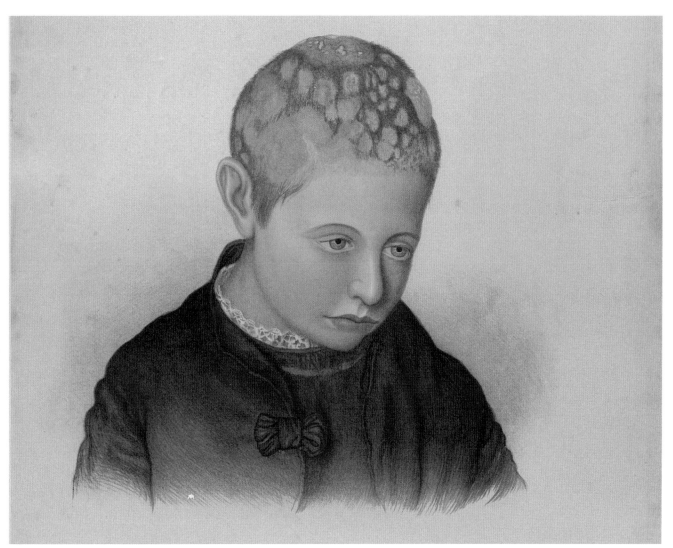

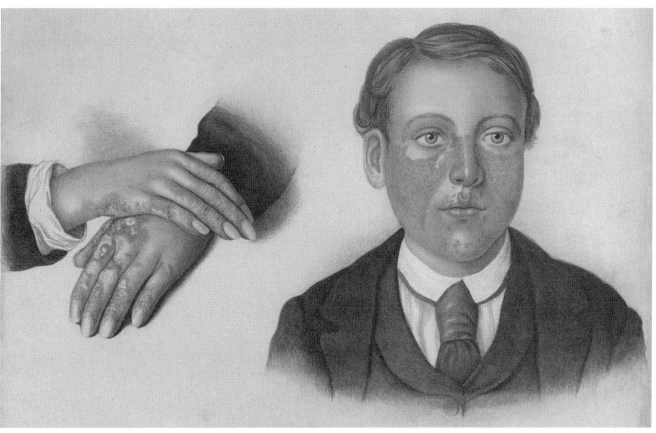

PLATE XLVII

CUT & COLLAGE

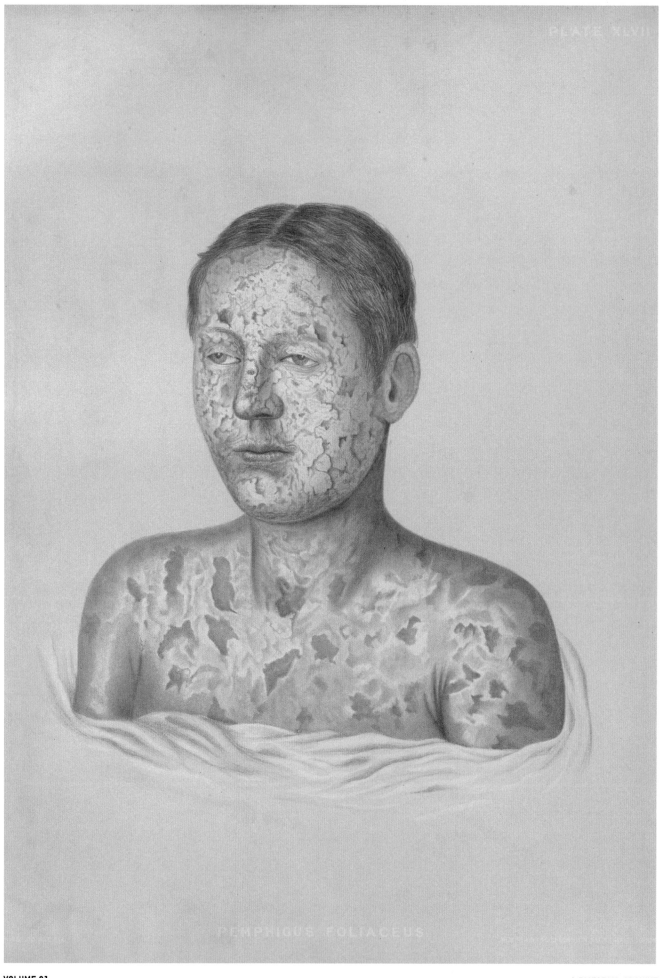

PEMPHIGUS FOLIACEUS

Plate XLII

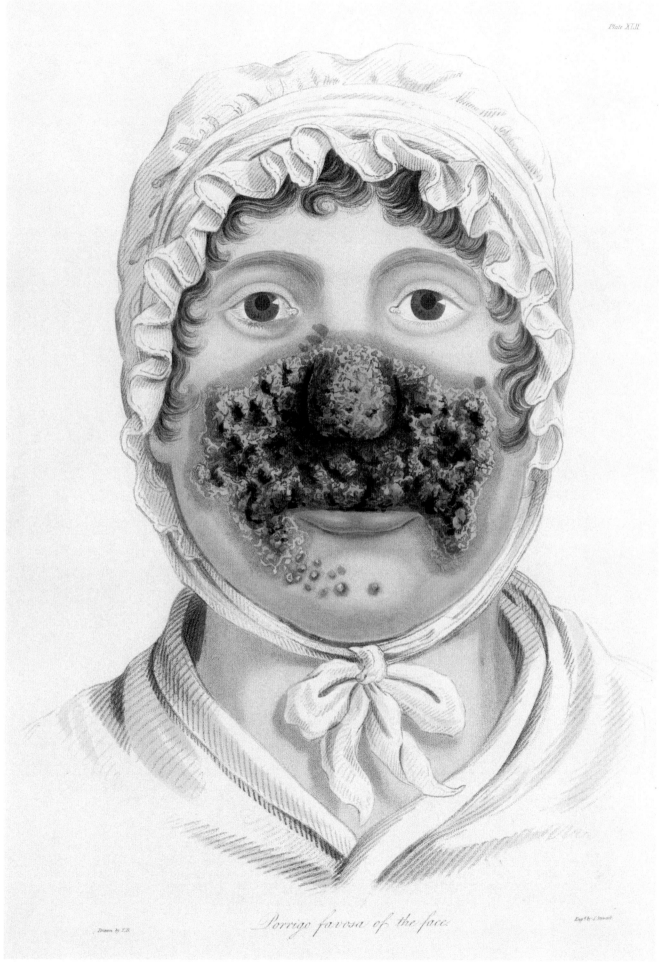

Drawn by T.B.   Porrigo favosa of the face.   Engᵈ by L. Stewart.

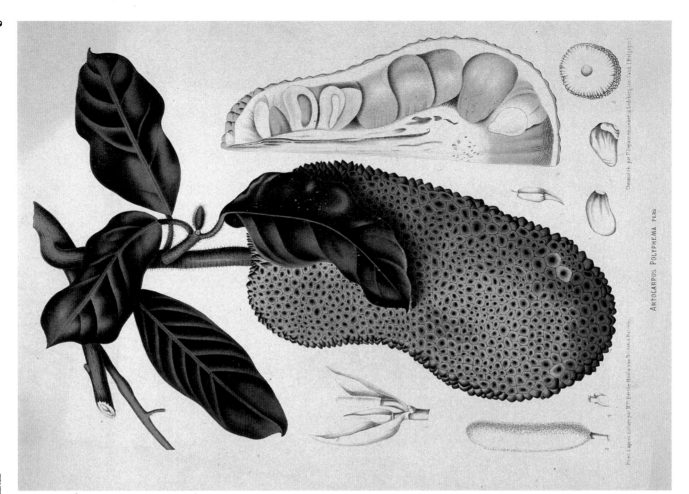

ARTOCARPUS POLYPHEMA PERS.

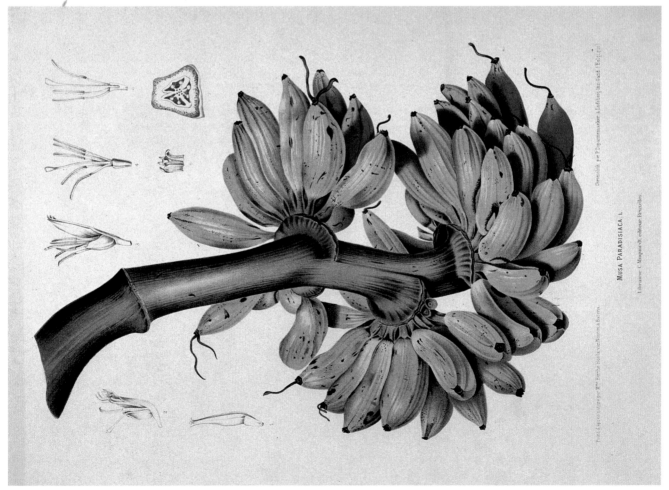

MUSA PARADISIACA L.

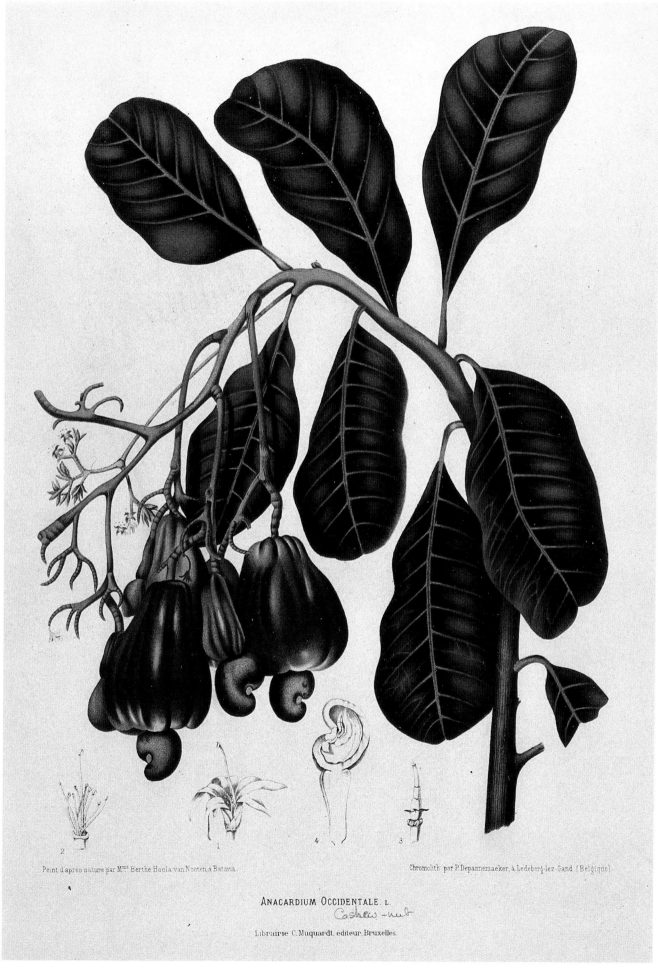

Peint d'apres nature par M.me Berthe Hoola van Nooten, a Batavia.

Chromolith par P.Depannemaeker, à Ledeberg-lez-Gand (Belgique)

ANACARDIUM OCCIDENTALE. L.

Cashew-nut

Librairie C.Muquardt, editeur, Bruxelles.

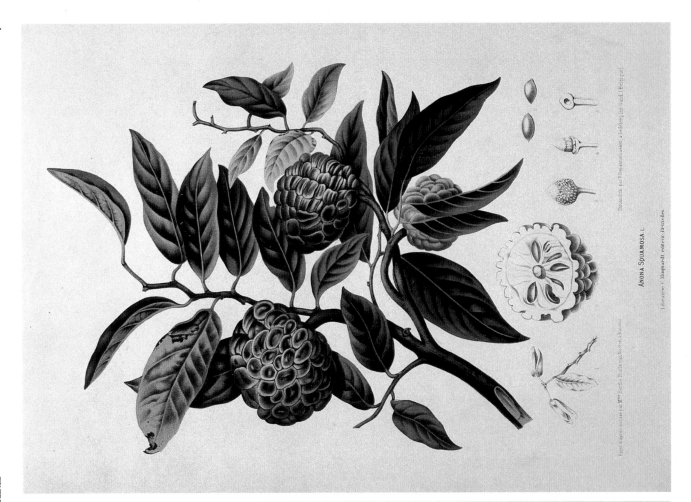

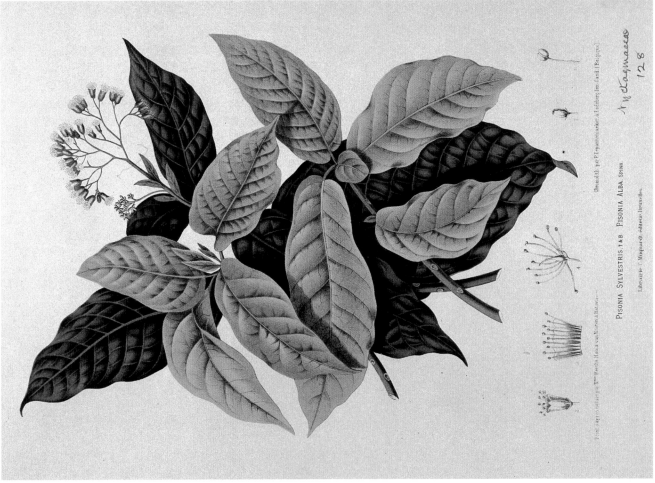

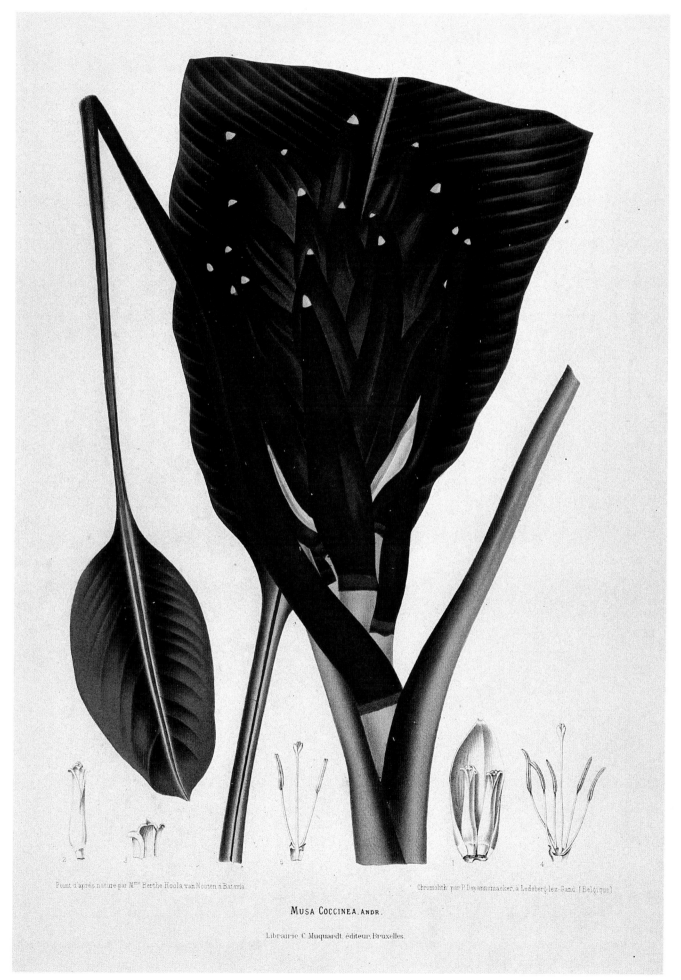

Peint d'après nature par Mme Berthe Hoola van Nouten, à Batavia.

Chromolith par P. Depannemaeker, à Ledeberg-lez-Gand (Belgique)

MUSA COCCINEA, ANDR.

Librairie C. Muquardt, éditeur, Bruxelles.

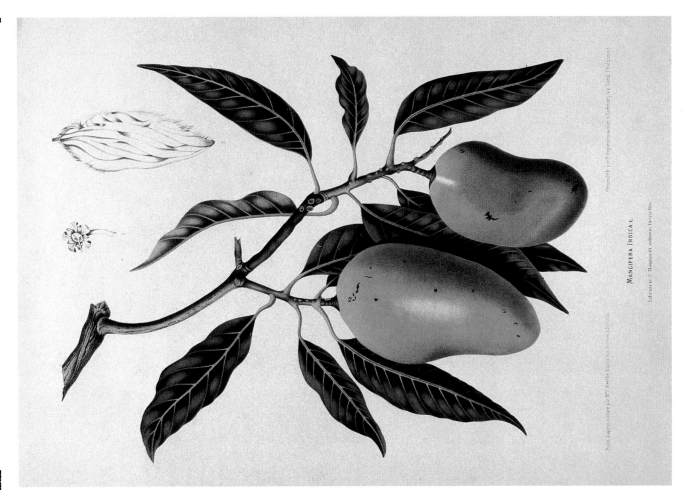

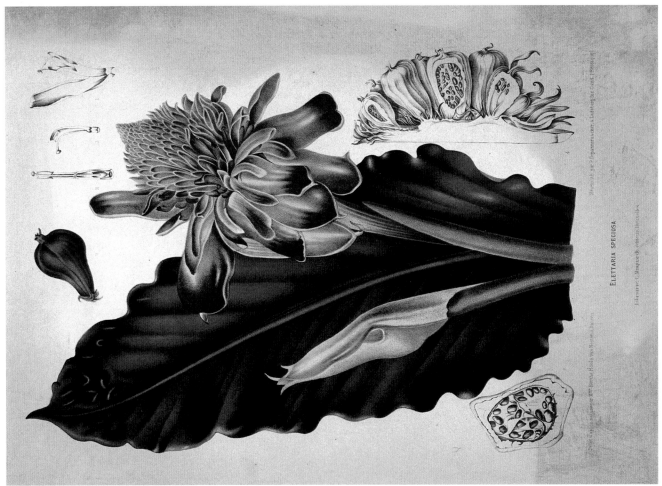

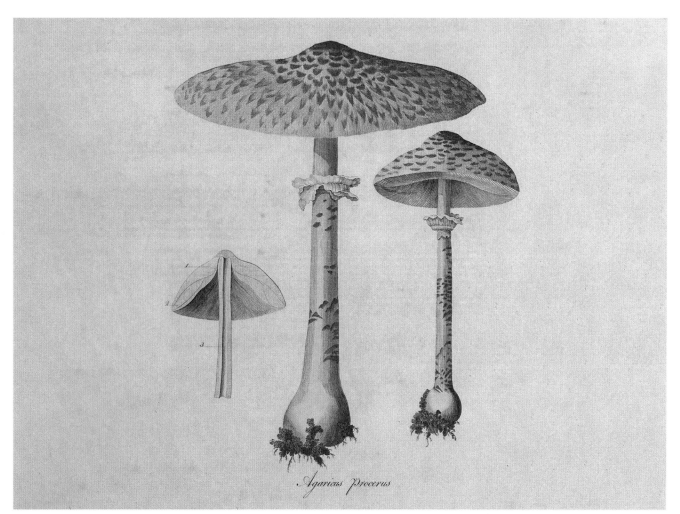

Agaricus Procerus

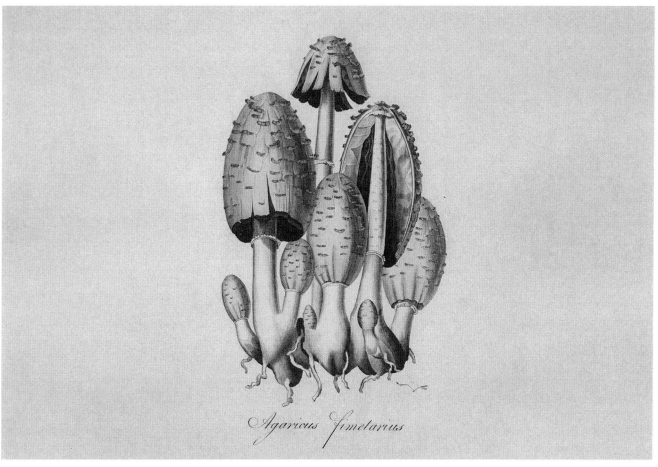

Agaricus fimetarius

CUT & COLLAGE

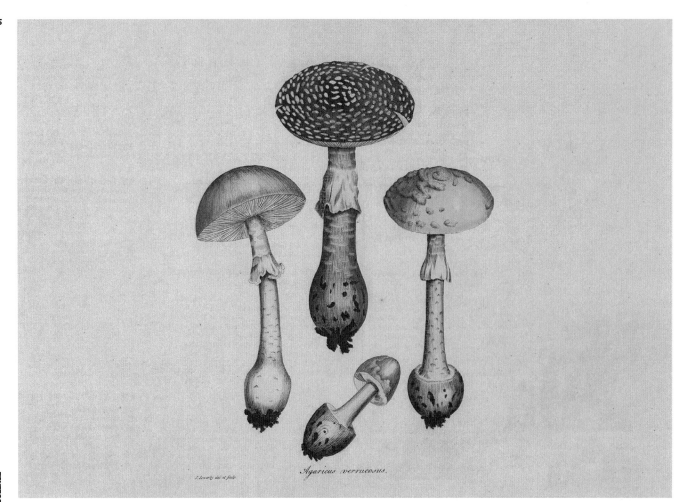

Agaricus verrucosus.

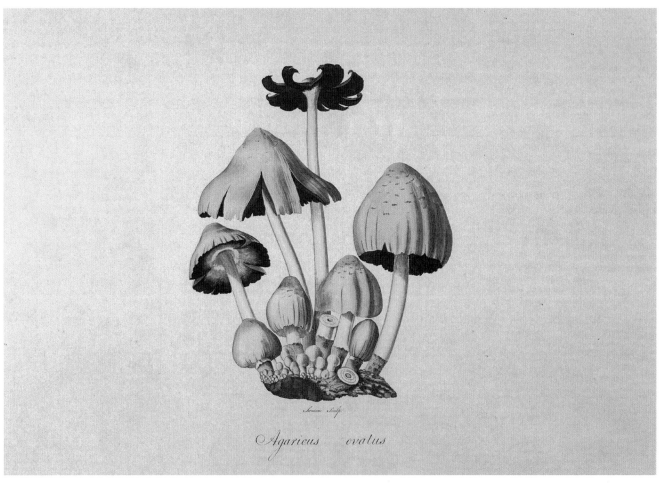

Agaricus ovatus

BLASIA, BOLETUS, BUXBAUMIA, AND BYSSUS.

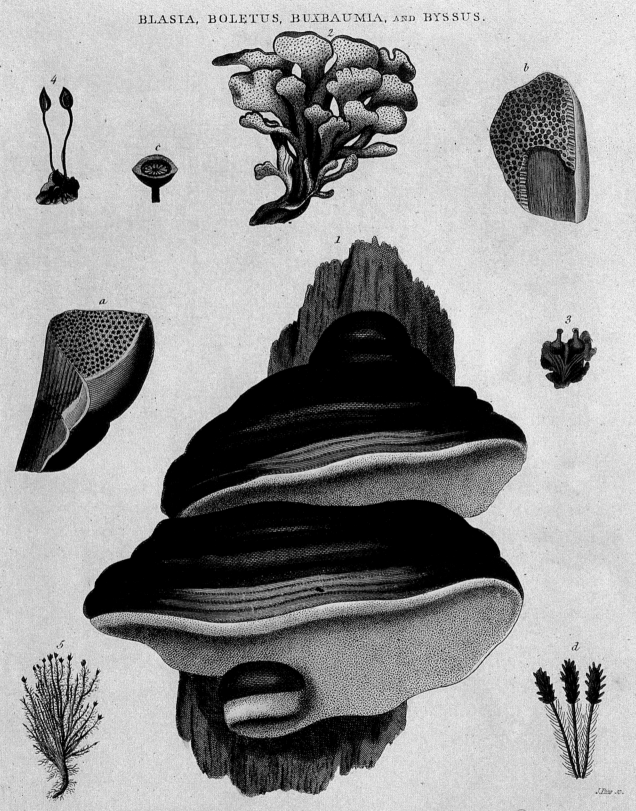

Fig.1. *Boletus igniarius*: a. *Section of the Pileus, to shew the tubulary pores*. 2. *Boletus frondosus*: b. *Section of the Pileus. magnified*. 3. *Blasia pusilla*. 4. *Buxbaumia aphylla*. c. *The Fruit-stalk. magnified*. 5. *Byssus fulva*. d. *Its Threads magnified*.

Published as the act directs, Jan. 24. 1809. by J. Wilkes.

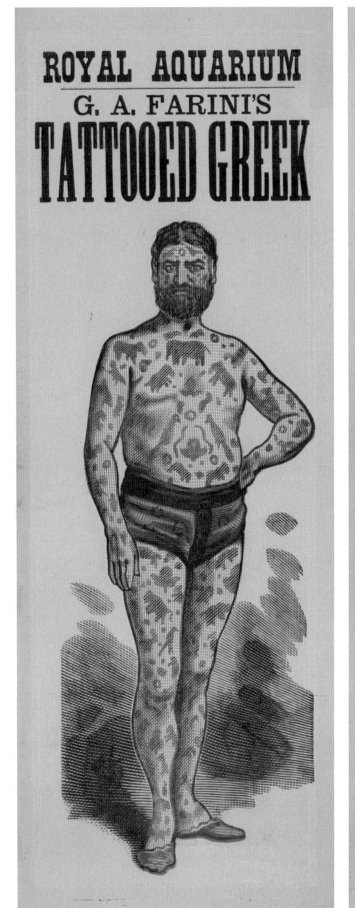

ROYAL AQUARIUM

G. A. FARINI'S

TATTOOED GREEK

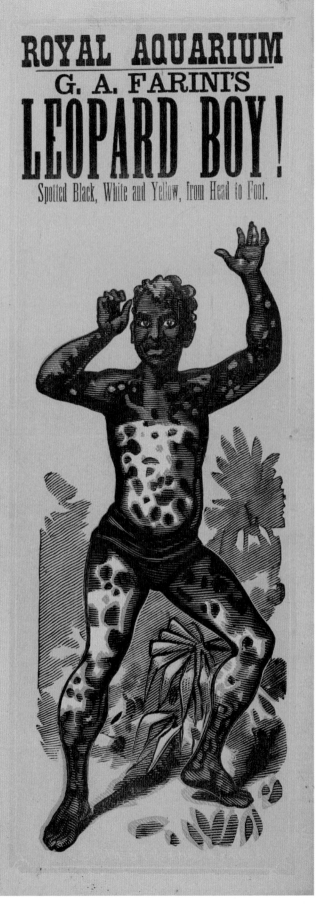

ROYAL AQUARIUM

G. A. FARINI'S

LEOPARD BOY!

Spotted Black, White and Yellow, from Head to Foot.

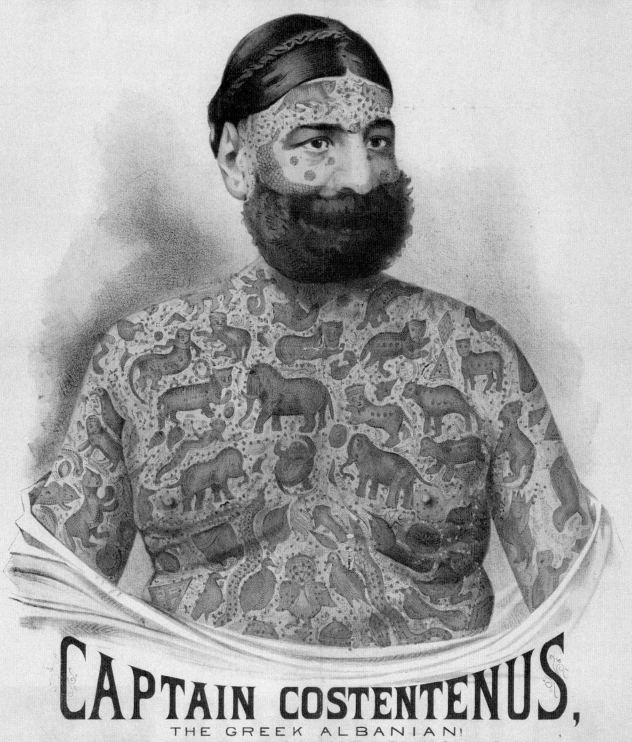

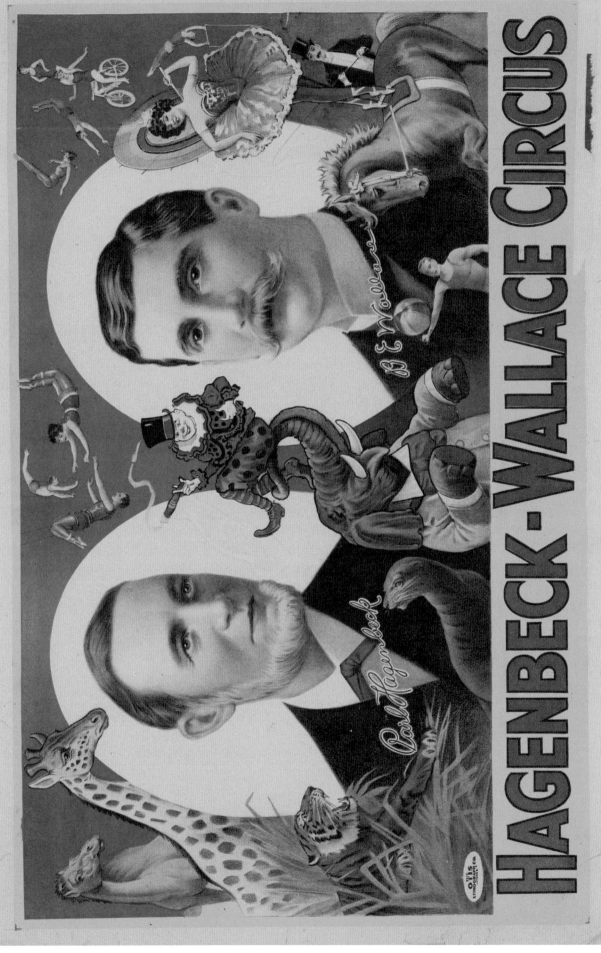

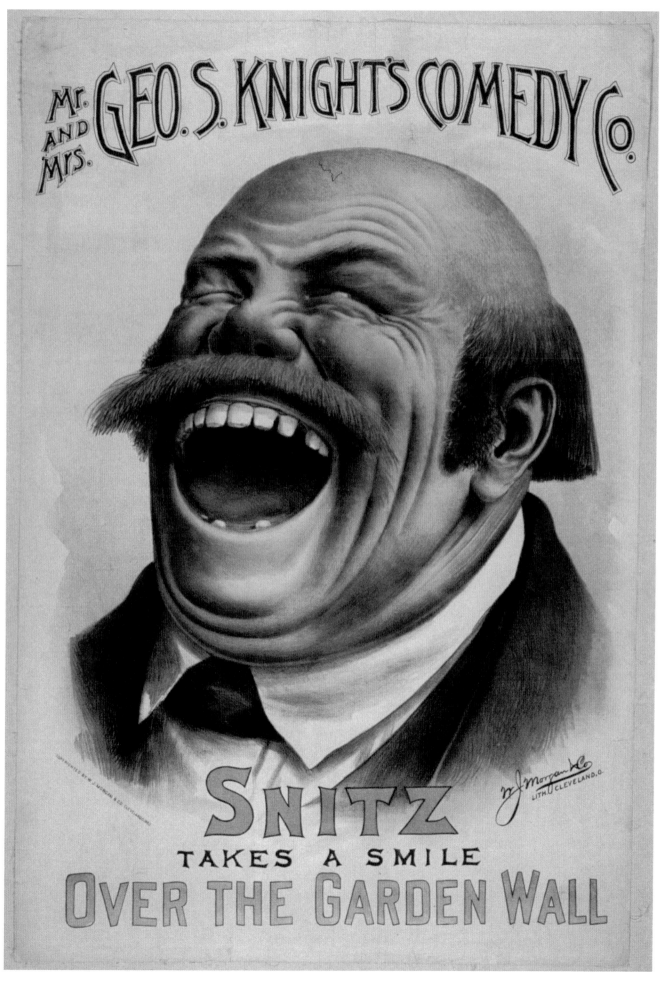

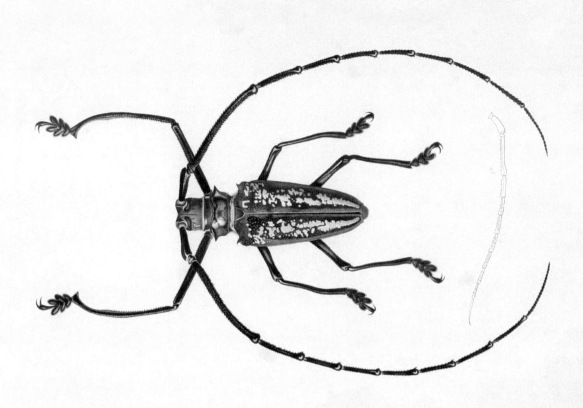

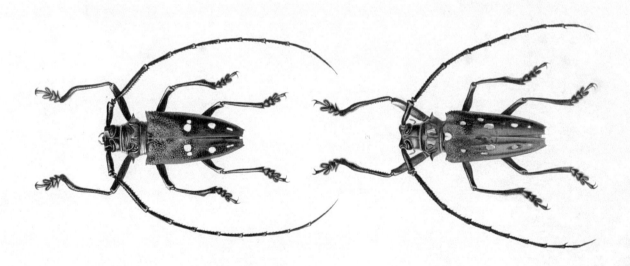

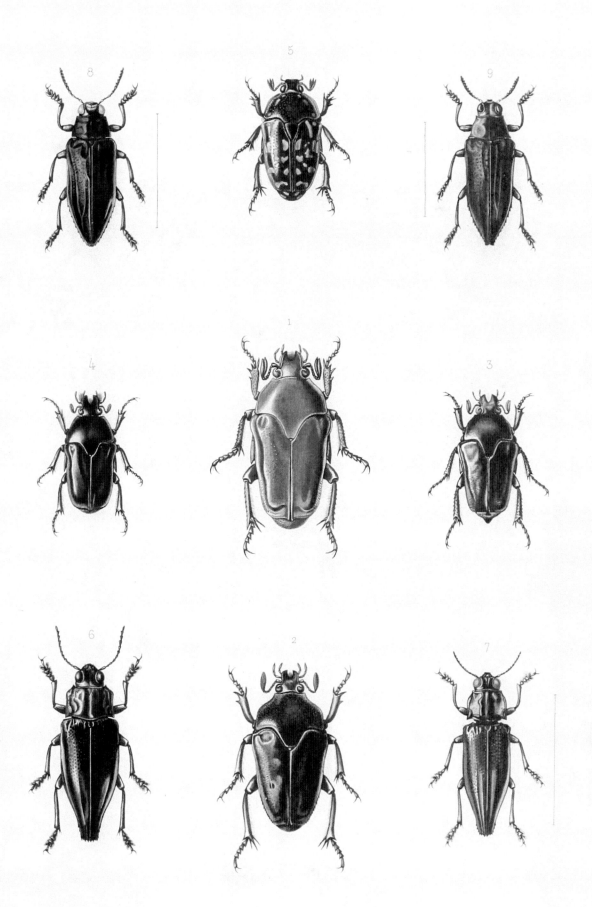

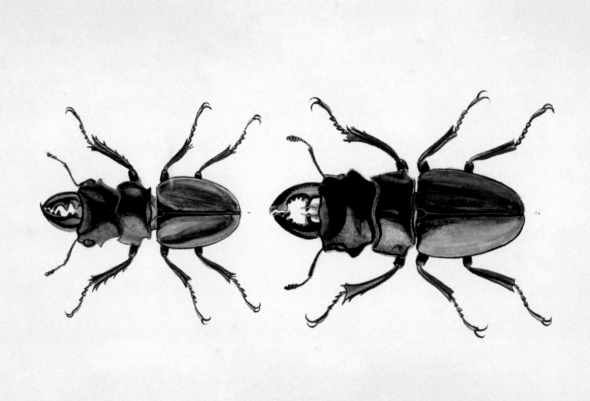

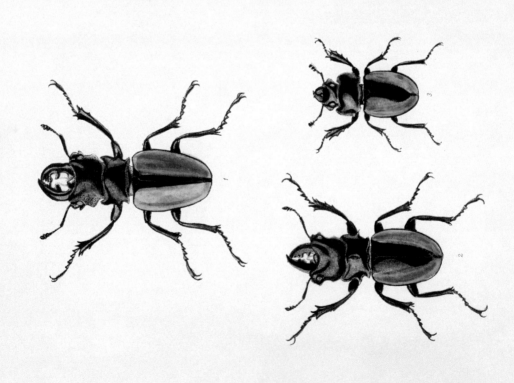

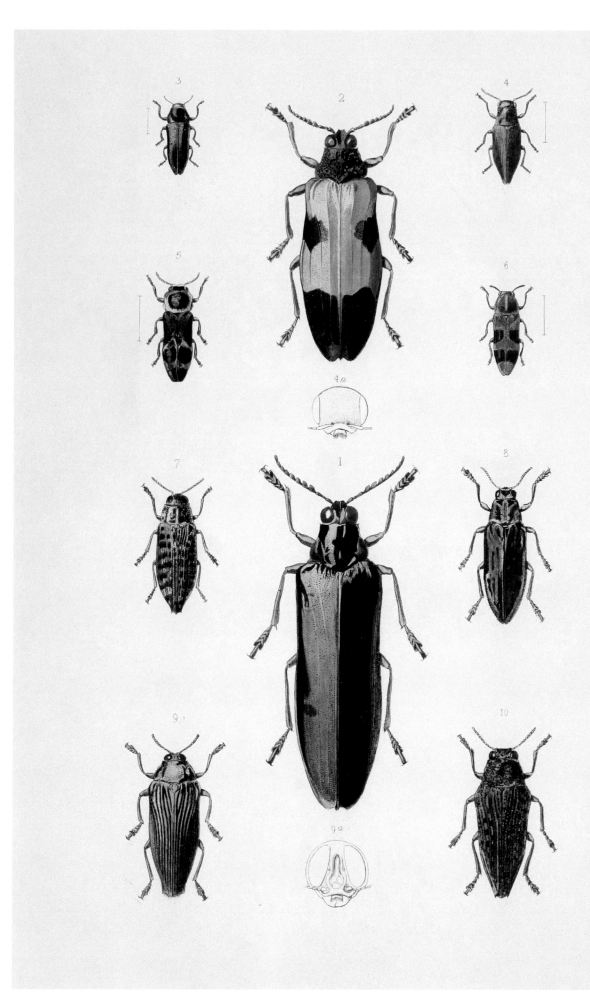

CUT & COLLAGE

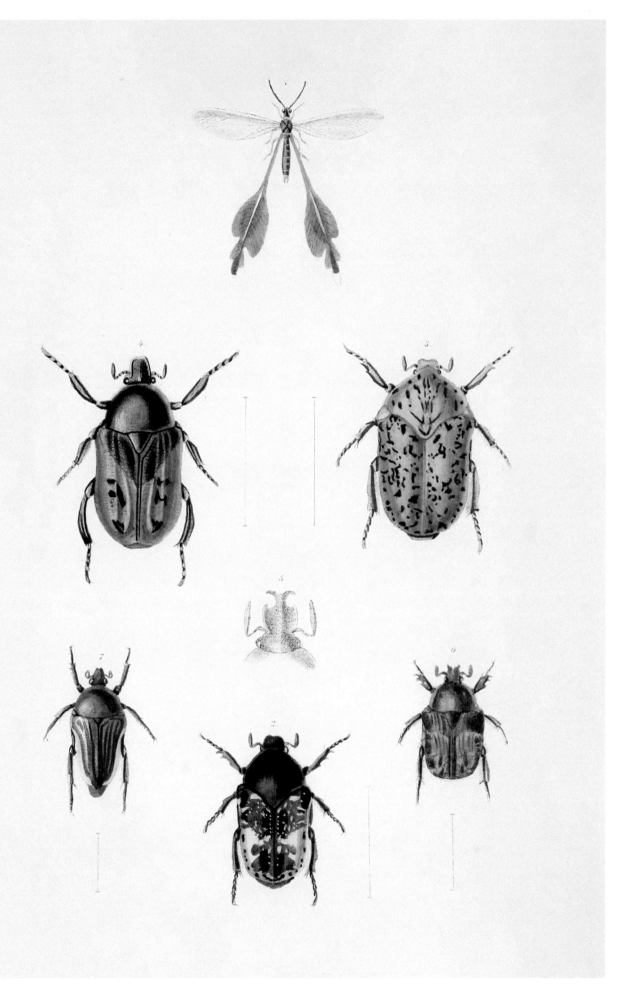

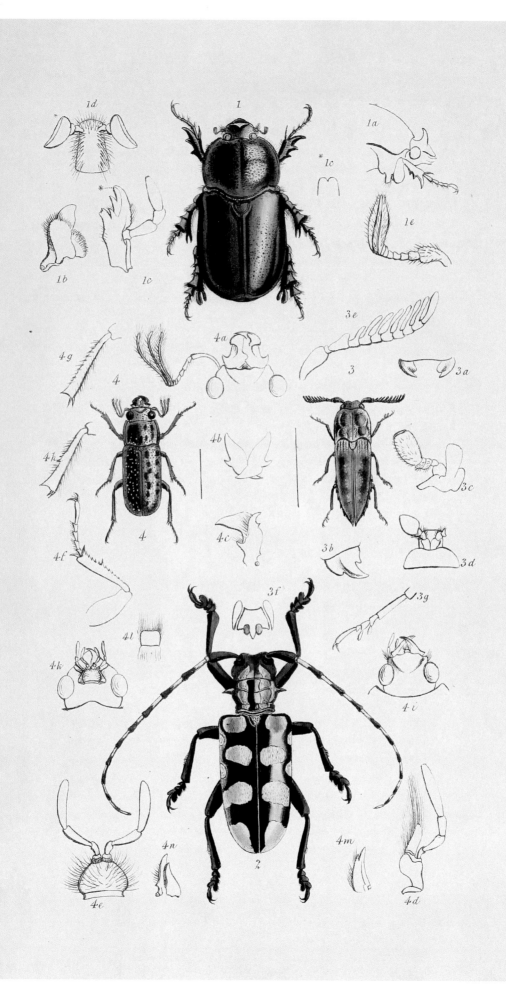

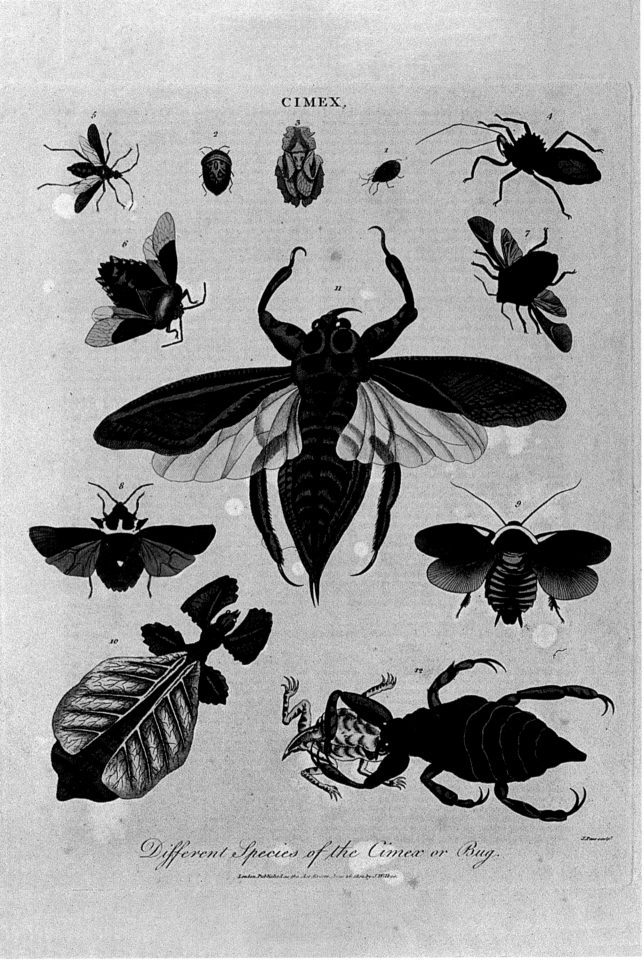

Different Species of the Cimex or Bug.

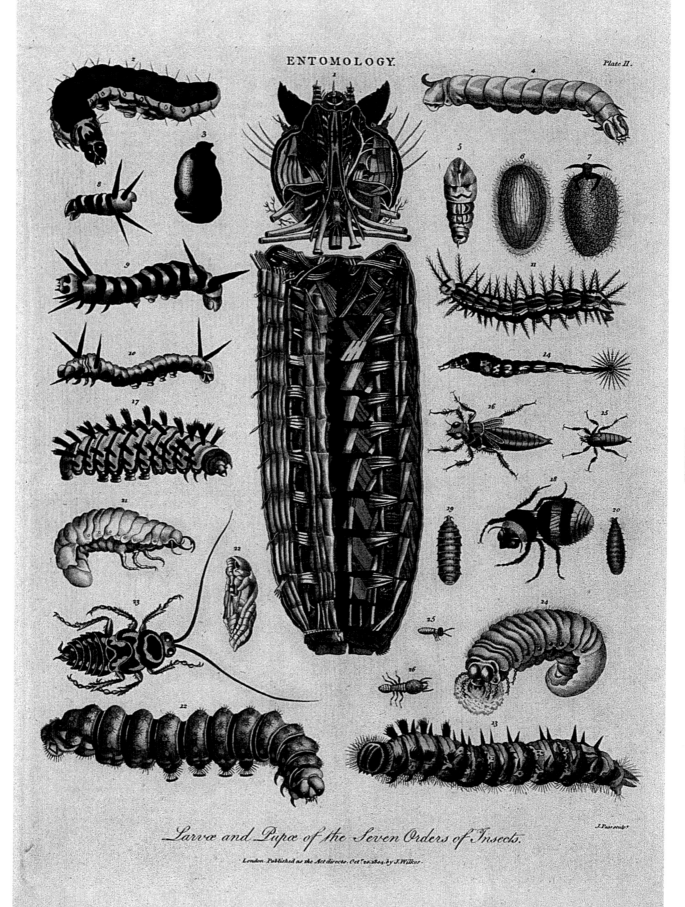

ENTOMOLOGY.

Plate II.

Larvæ and Pupæ of the Seven Orders of Insects.

London. Published as the Act directs. Oct.ʳ 25.1804. by J.Wilker.

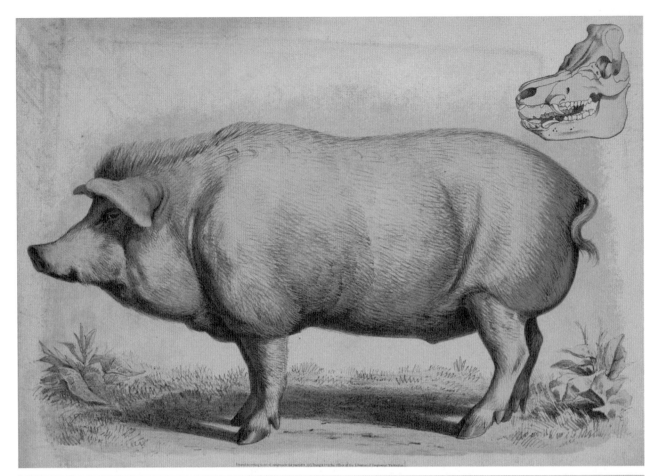

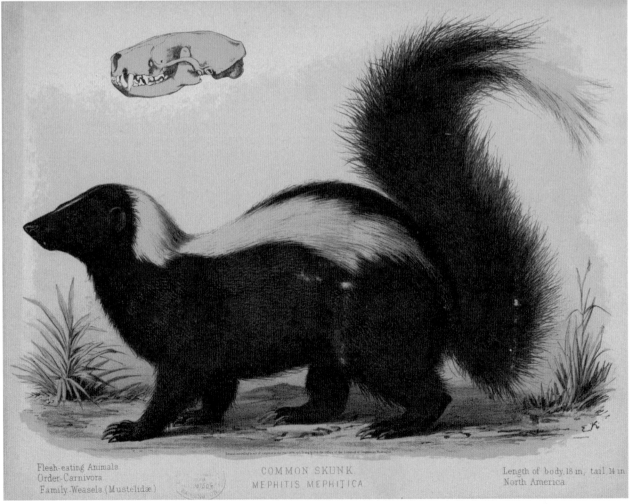

Flesh-eating Animals
Order-Carnivora
Family-Weasels (Mustelidæ)

COMMON SKUNK
MEPHITIS MEPHITICA

Length of body, 18 in, tail, 14 in
North America

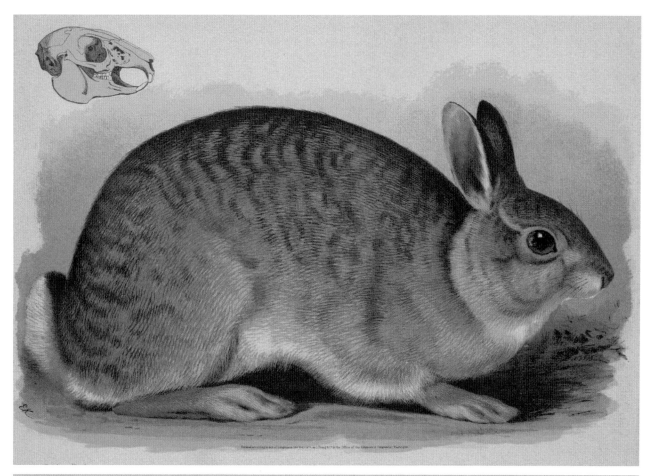

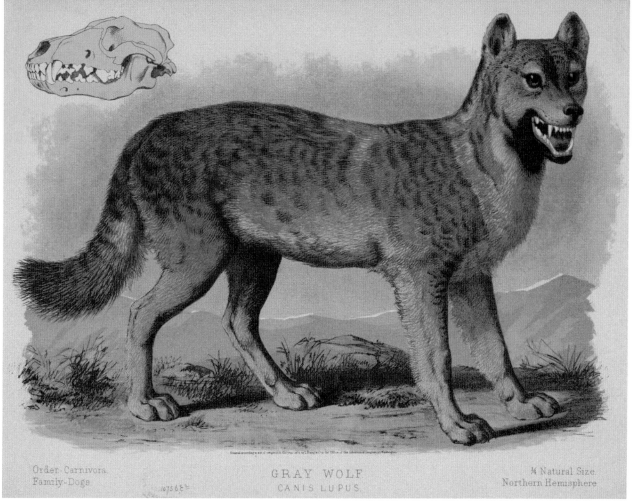

Order-Carnivora.
Family-Dogs.

GRAY WOLF
CANIS LUPUS.

¾ Natural Size.
Northern Hemisphere

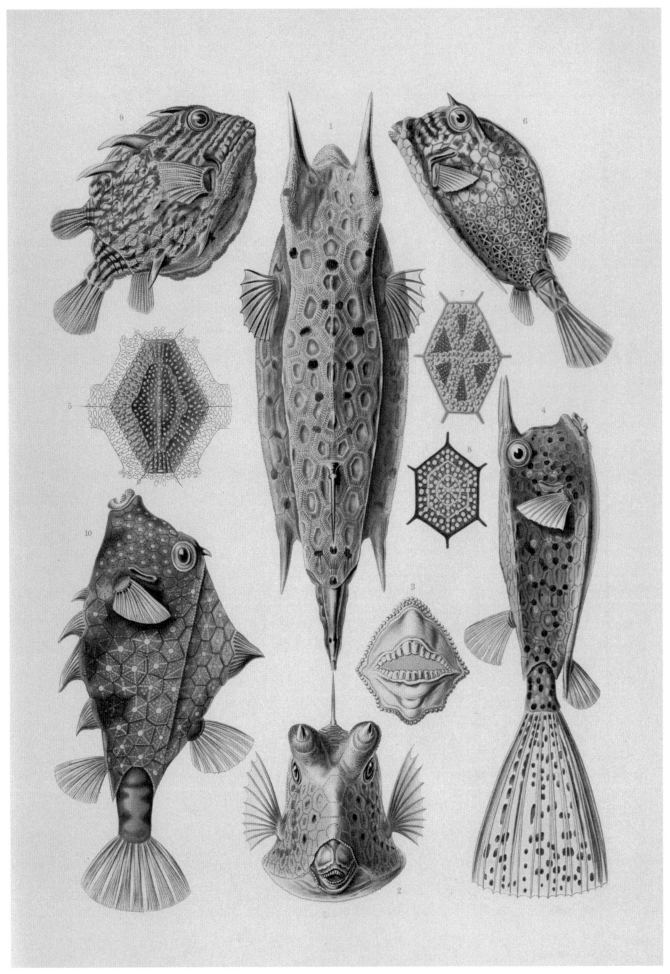

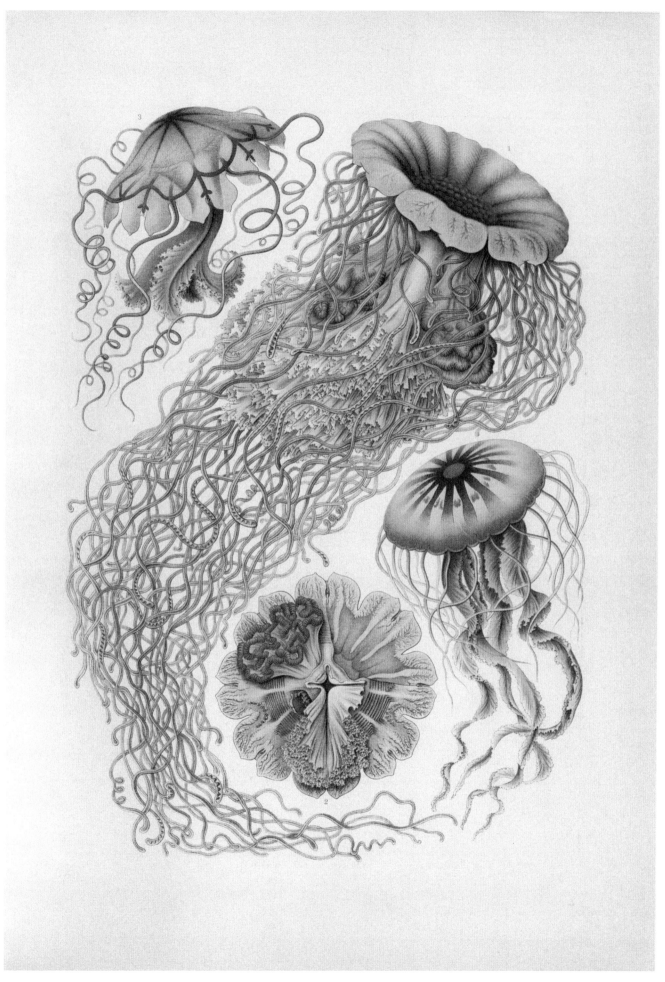

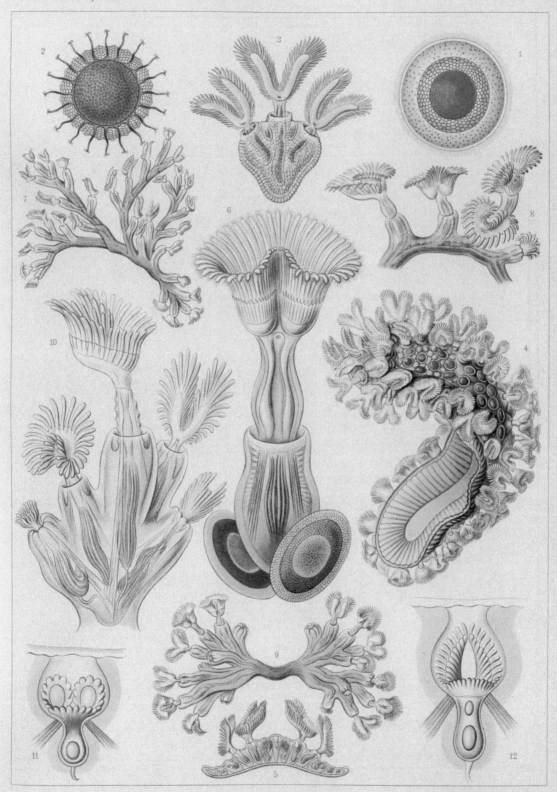

Bryozoa. — Moostiere.

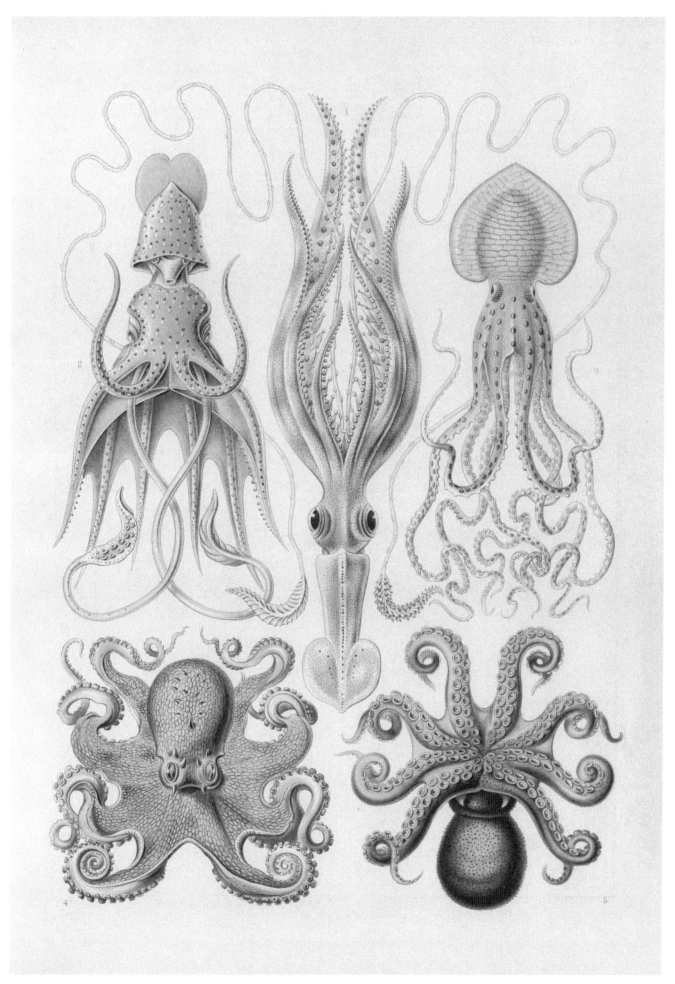

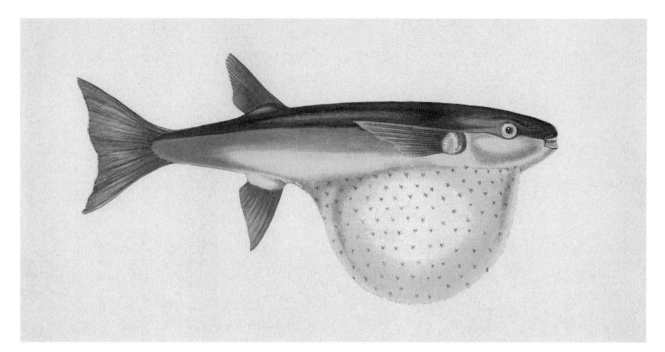

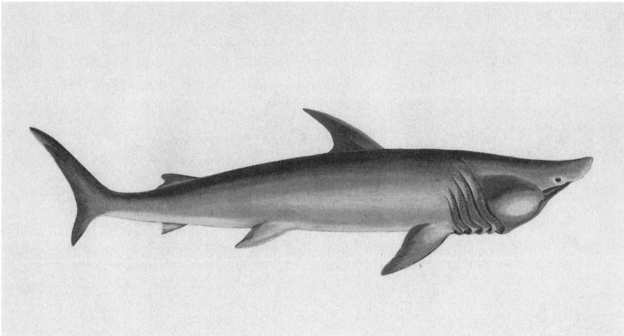

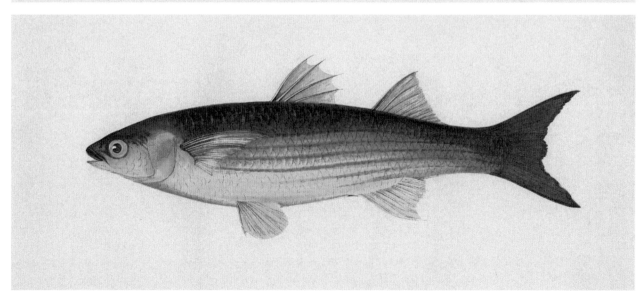

CUT & COLLAGE

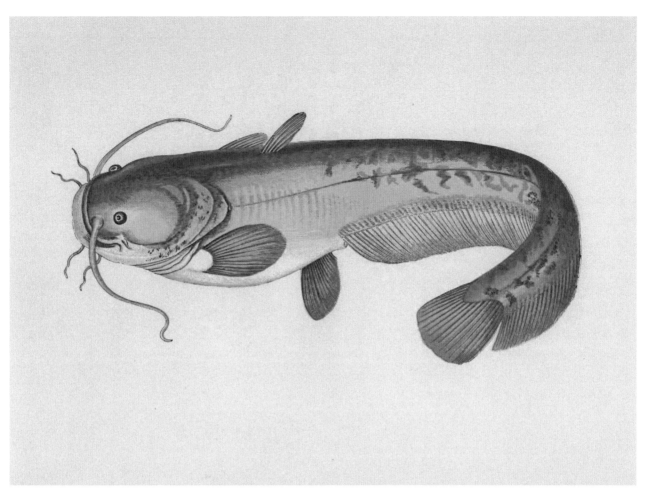

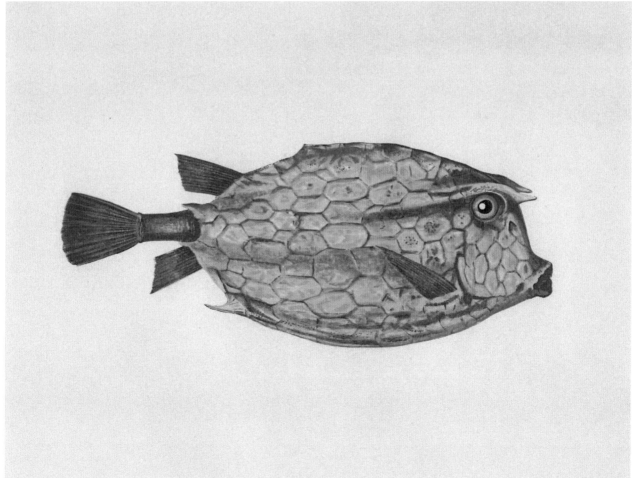

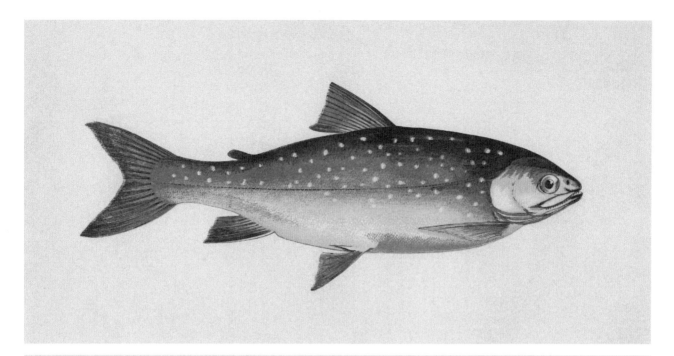

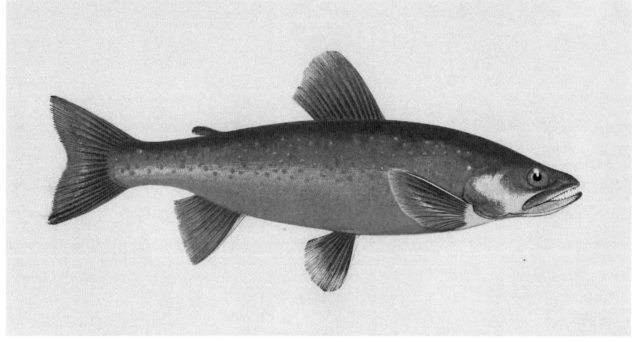

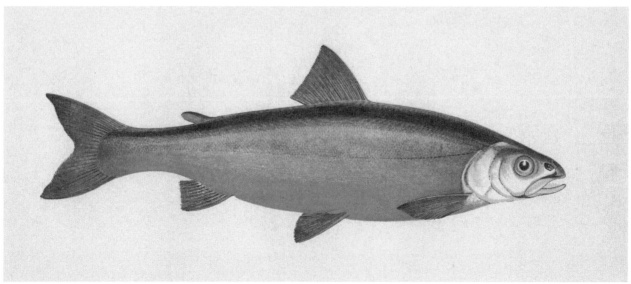

CUT & COLLAGE

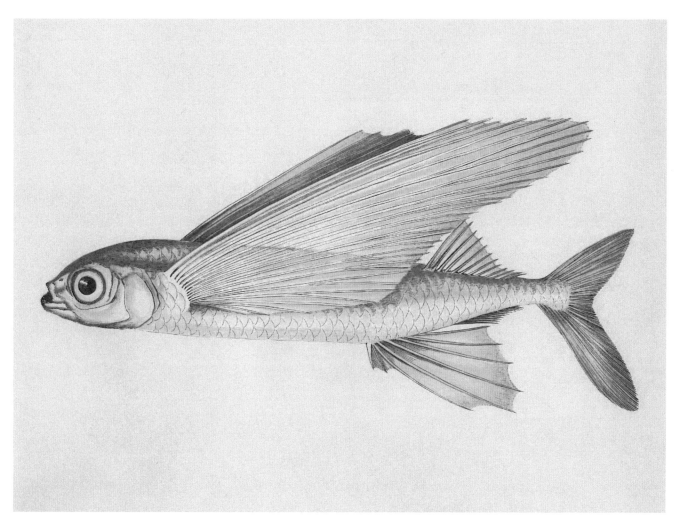

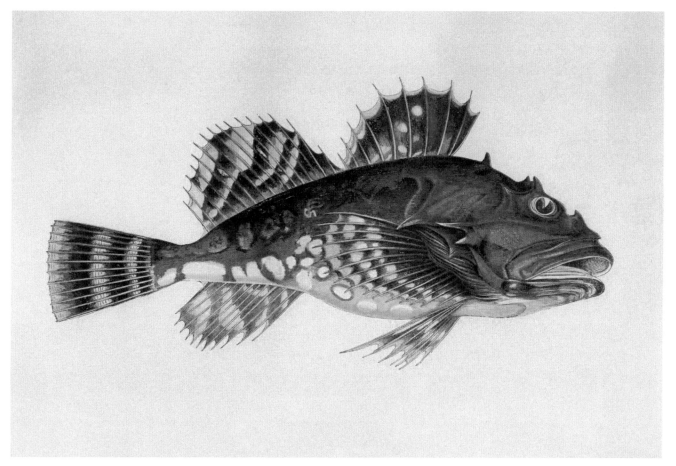

DIODON.

Plate II.

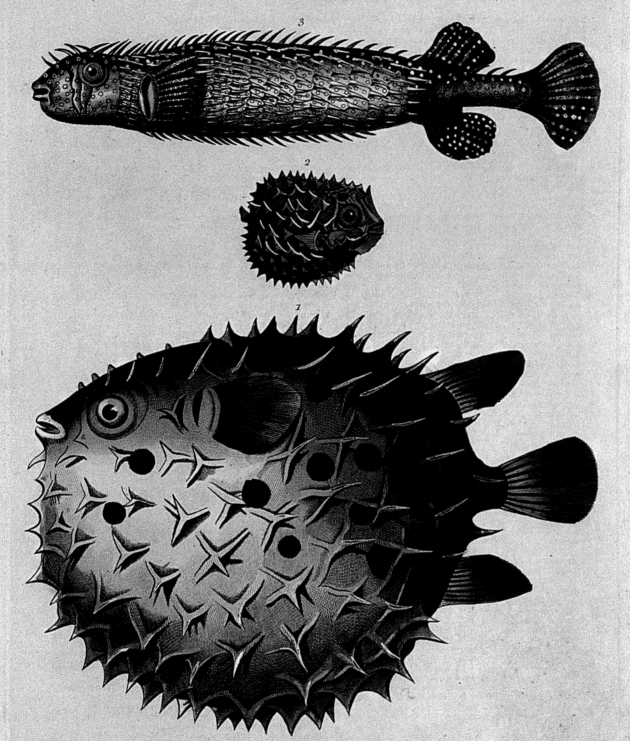

1. The orbicular Diodon or Bottle fish. 2. The Mole Diodon. 3. Plumiers Diodon.

MONODON AND MONSTER.

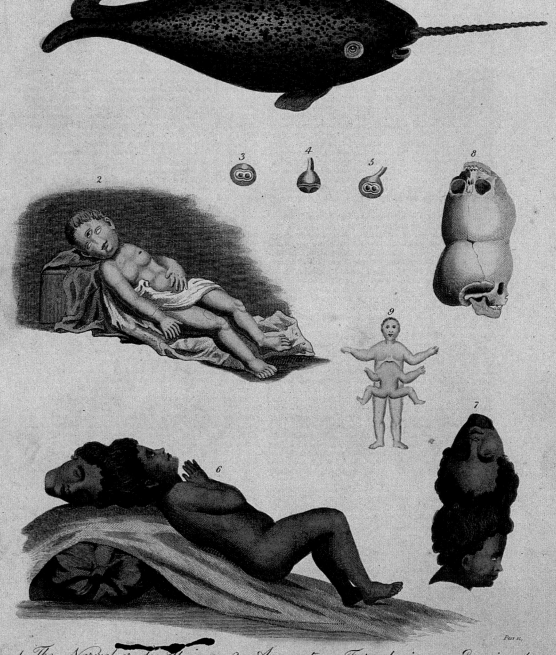

1. The Narval or Sea Unicorn. 2. A monstrous Fœtus having an Eye in the middle of the Forehead. 6. A Child with two Heads. 9. A double Child.

Engraved for the Encyclopædia London 1817.

TAB. CAP. XIII.

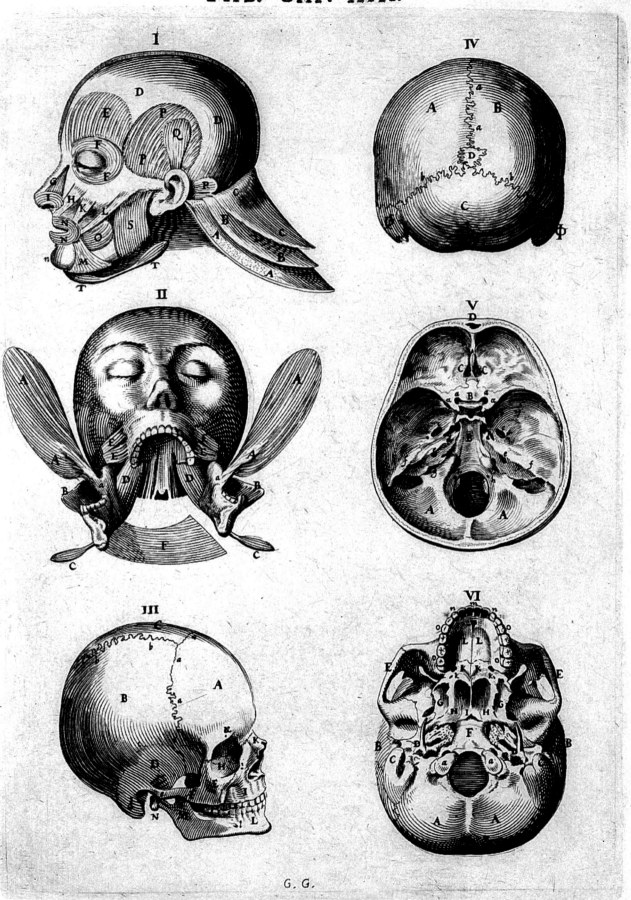

G. G.

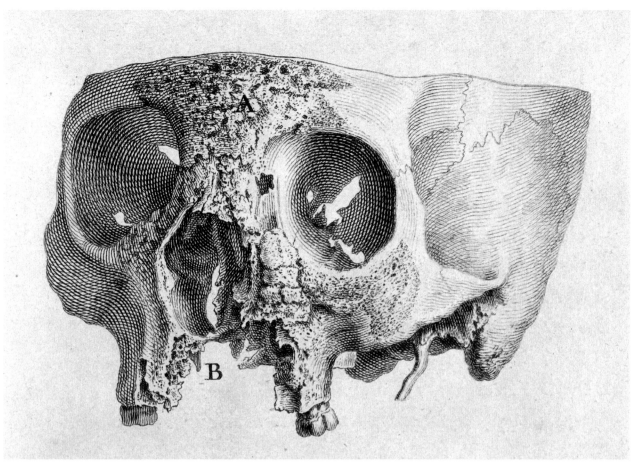

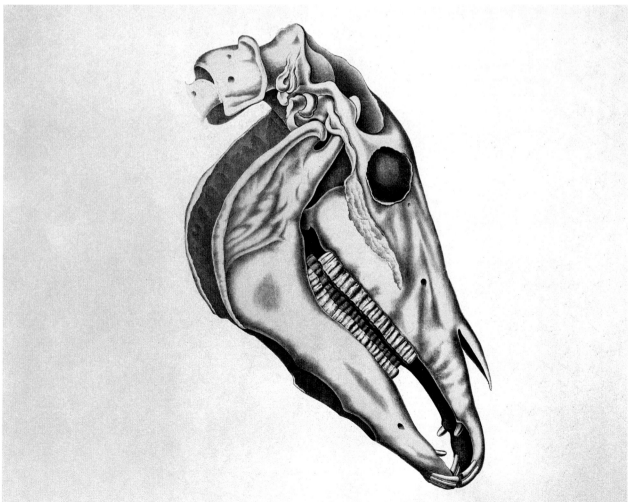

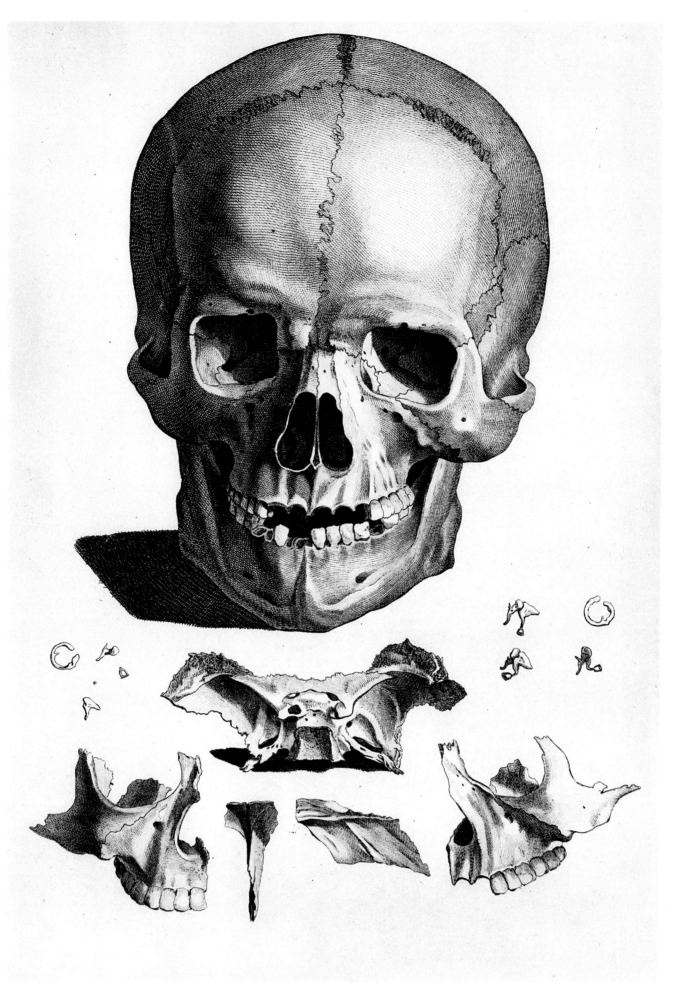

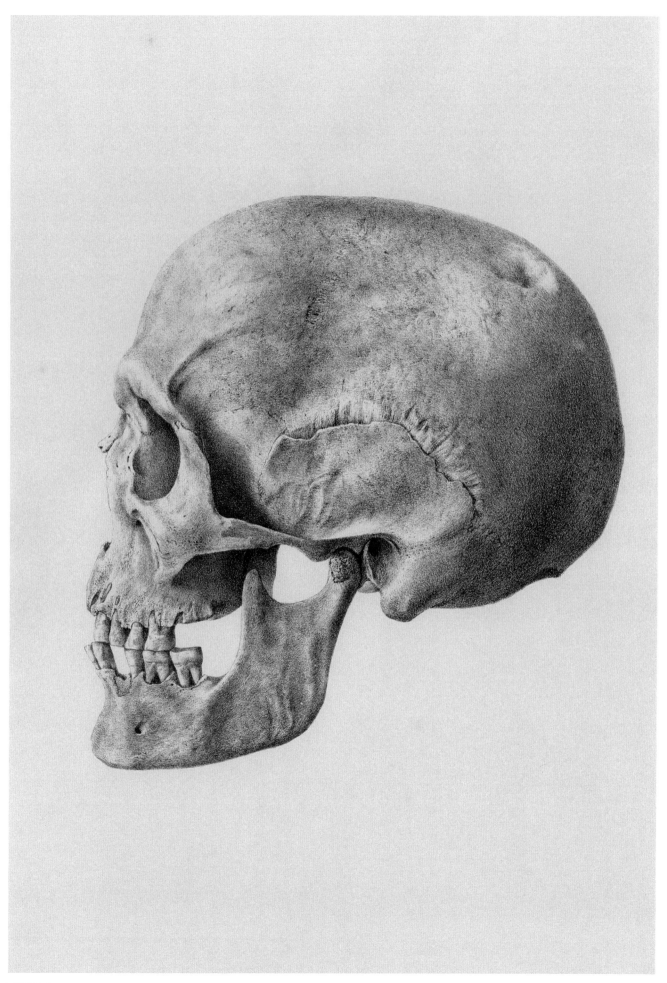

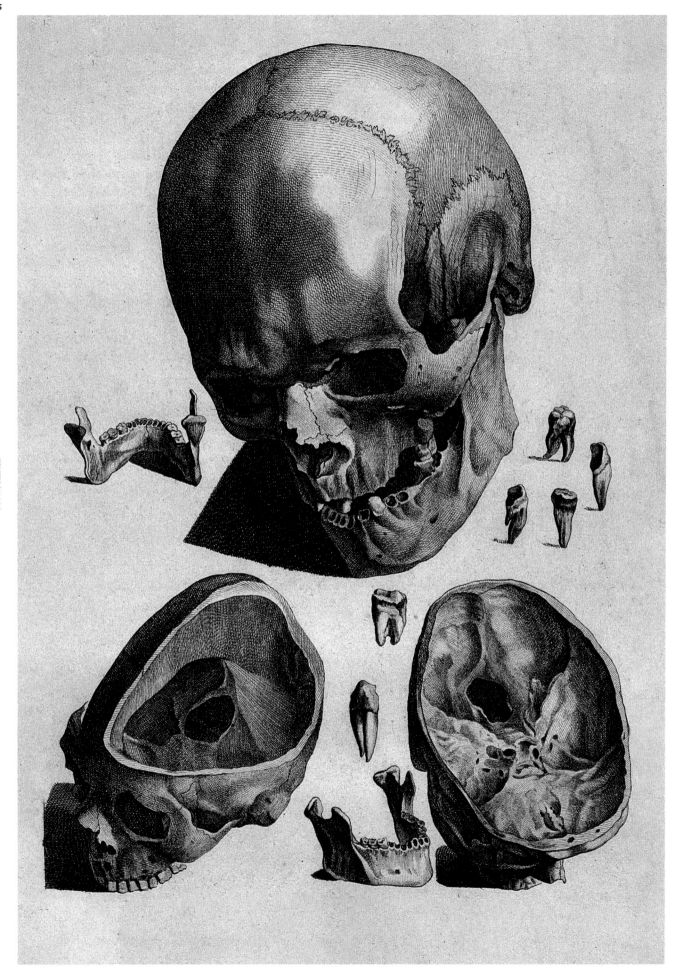

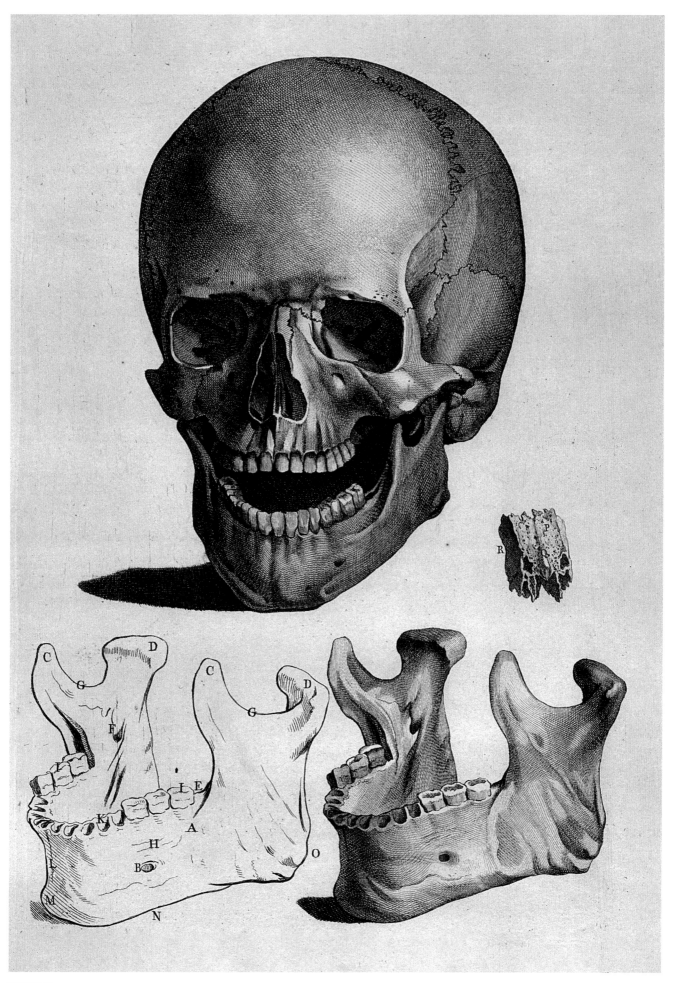

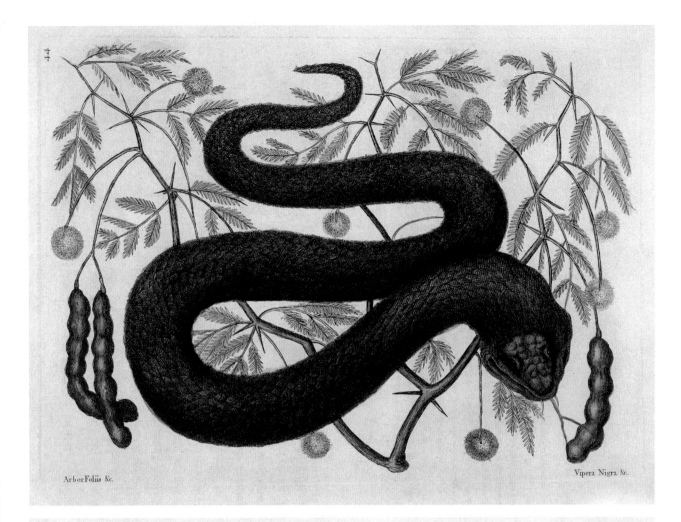

ArborFoliis &c.

Vipera. Nigra. &c.

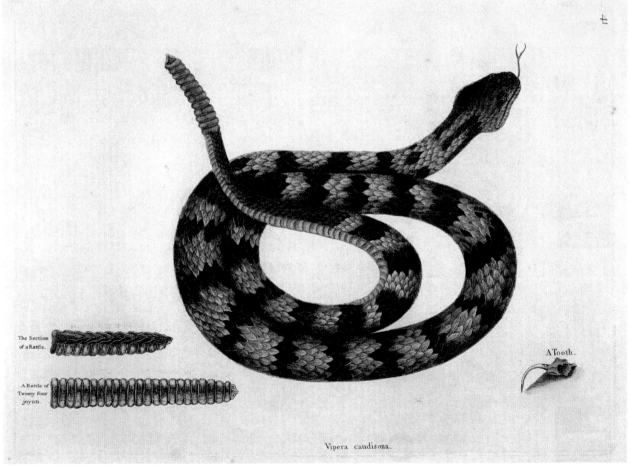

The Section
of a Rattle.

A Rattle of
Twenty four
joynts.

A Tooth.

Vipera caudisona.

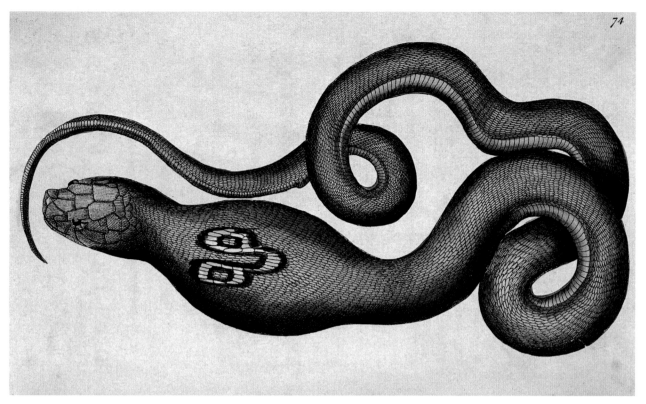

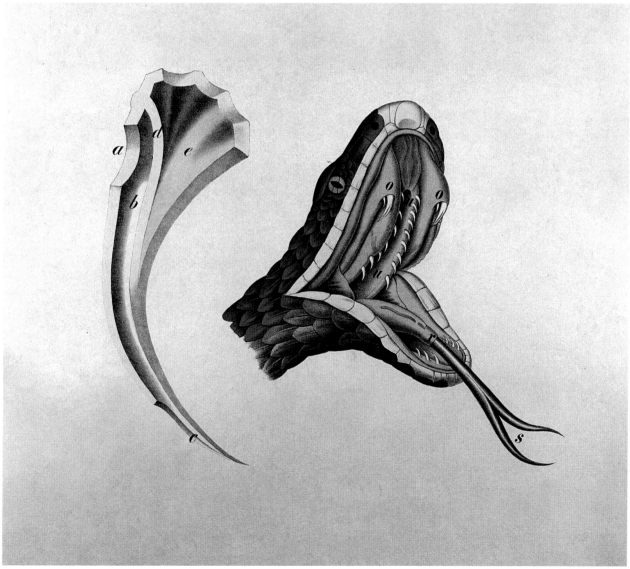

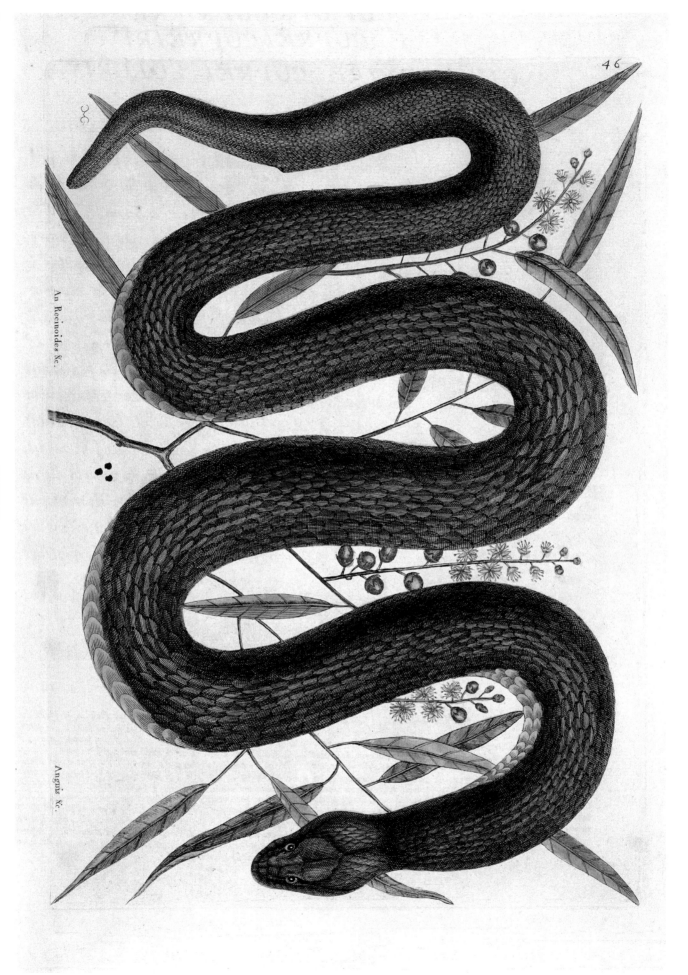

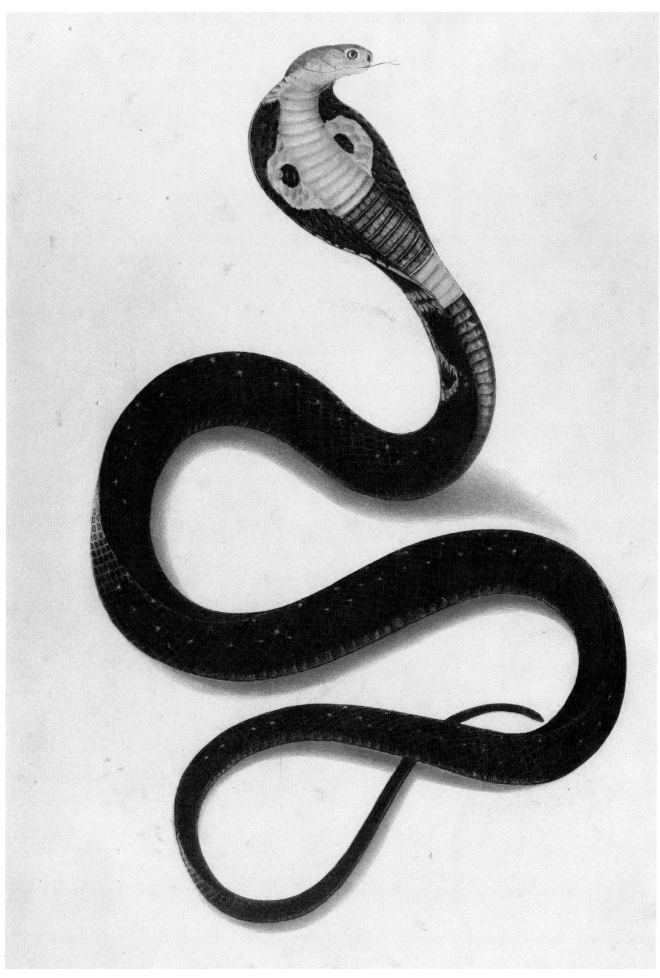

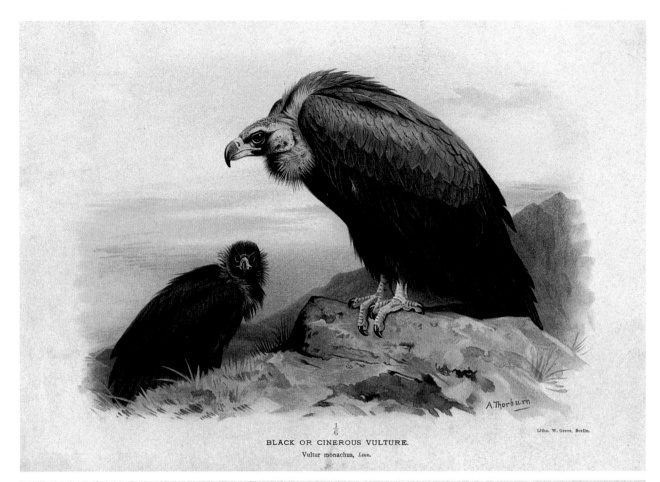

$\frac{1}{6}$

BLACK OR CINEROUS VULTURE.

Vultur monachus, *Linn.*

Litho. W. Greve, Berlin.

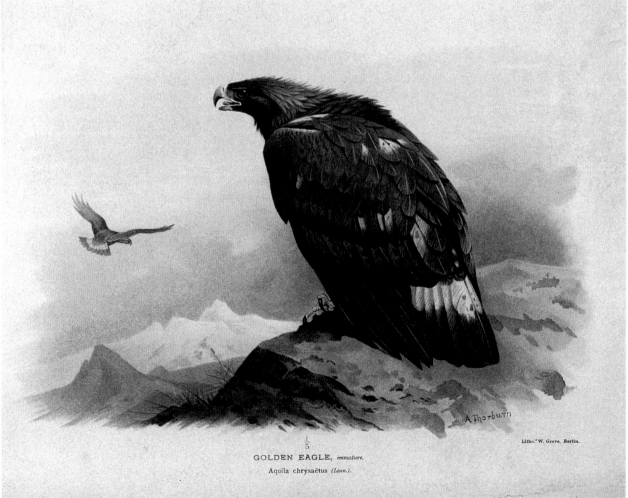

$\frac{1}{5}$

GOLDEN EAGLE, *immature.*

Aquila chrysaëtus (*Linn.*).

Litho. W. Greve, Berlin.

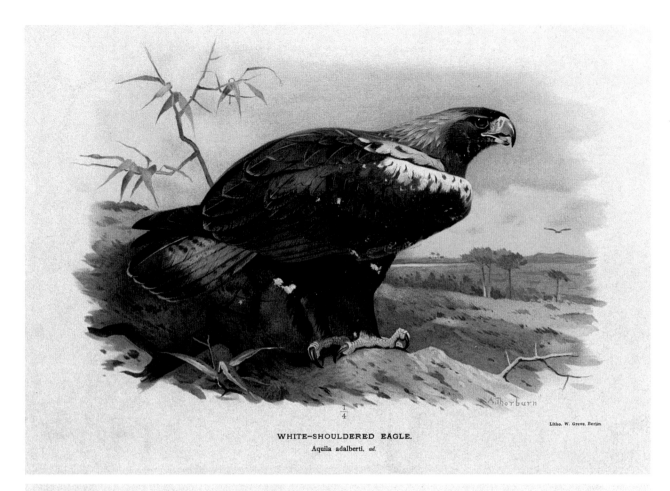

$\frac{1}{4}$

Litho. W. Greve, Berlin.

WHITE–SHOULDERED EAGLE.

Aquila adalberti, *ad.*

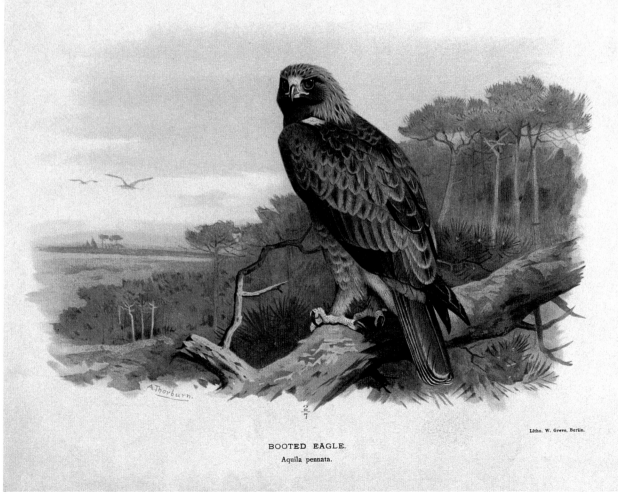

$\frac{2}{7}$

Litho. W. Greve, Berlin.

BOOTED EAGLE.

Aquila pennata.

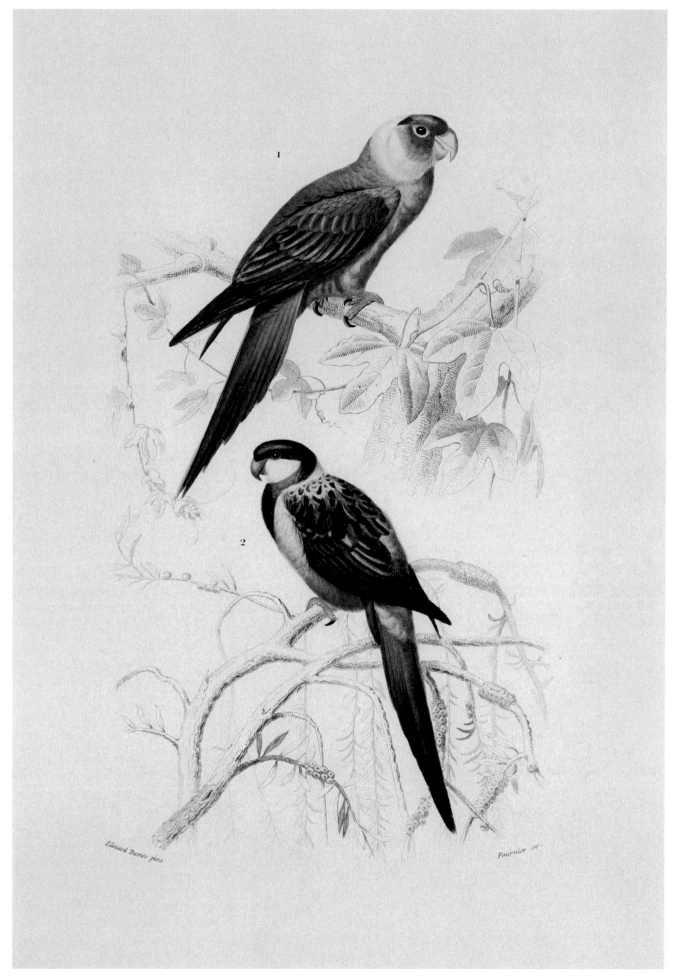

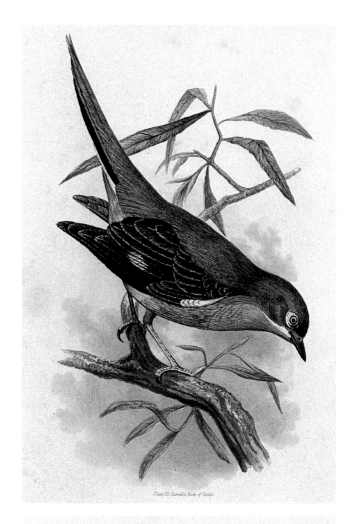

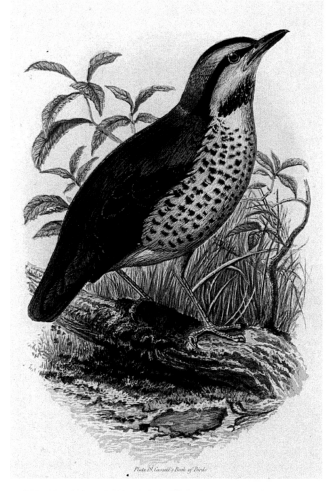

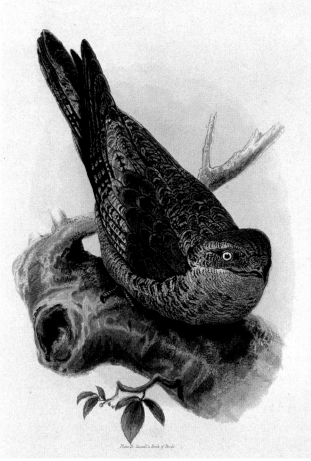

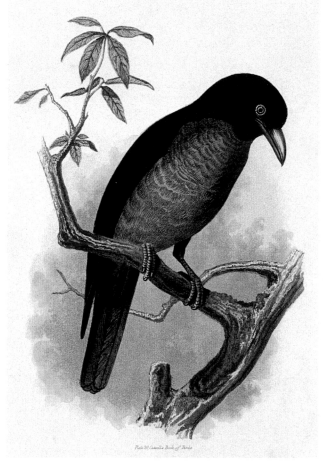

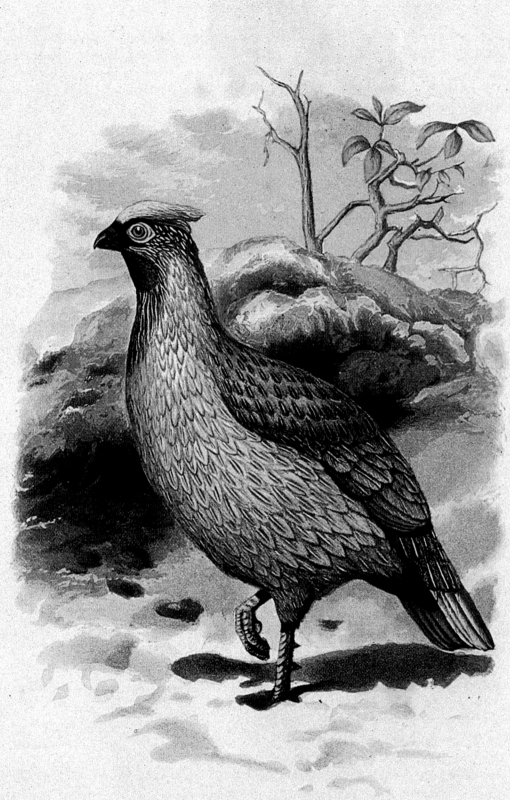

Plate 29. Cassell's Book of Birds

ITHAGINIS CORIENTES _____ SANGUINE FRANCOLIN

(about one half Nat. size)

Plate 6_Ornithology

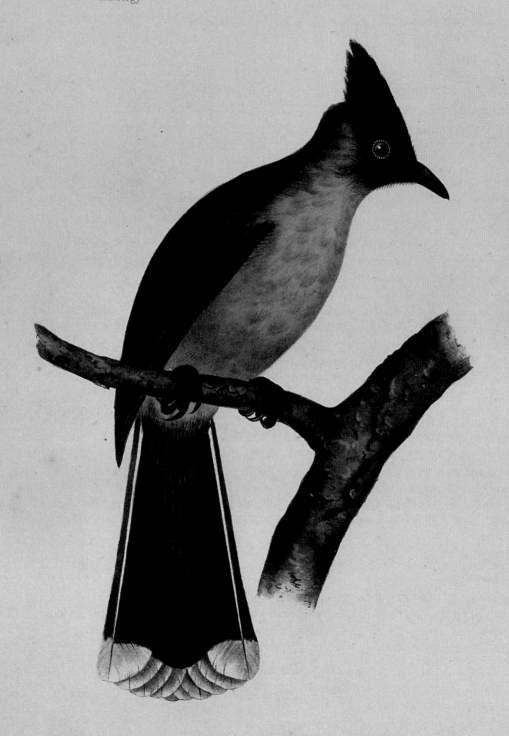

IXOS HAEMORRHOUS __ GMELIN

Lith of Wᵐ E Hitchcock, Philadª

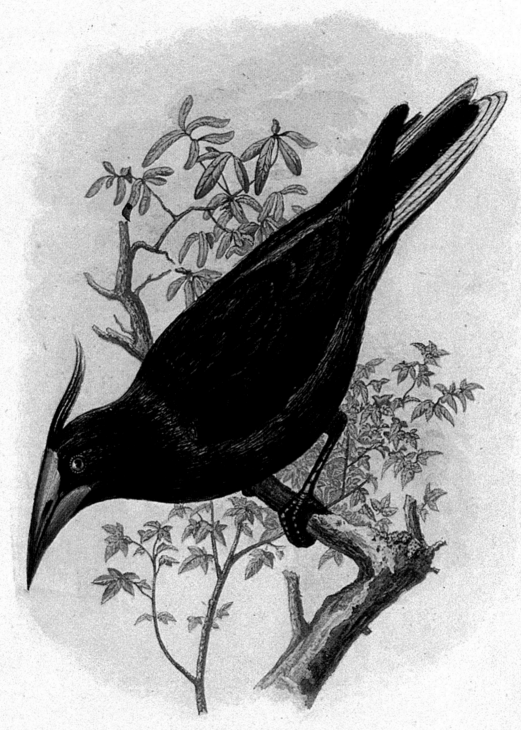

Plate 6, Cassell's Book of Birds

WAGLERS CASSICUS ———— Cassicus Wagleri

(Three-fourths Life size)

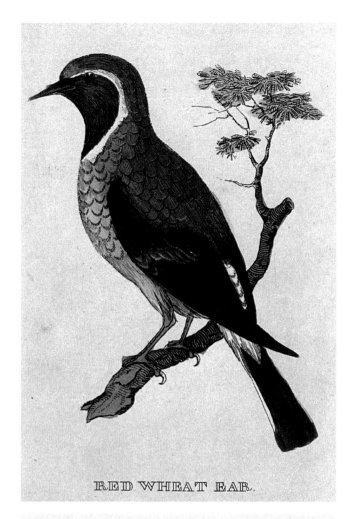

RED WHEAT EAR.

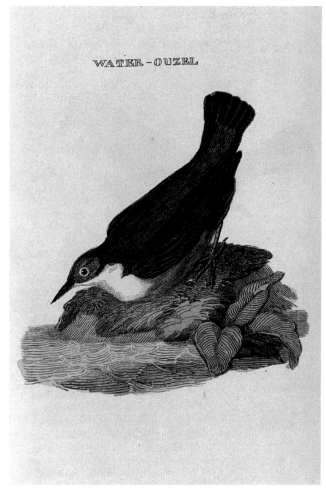

WATER-OUZEL

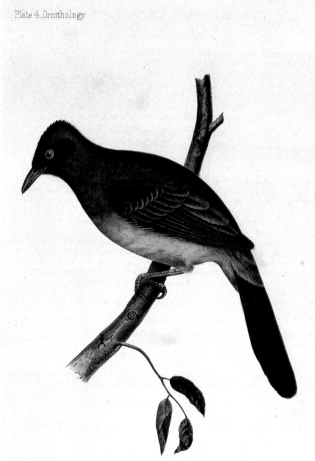

Plate 4. Ornithology.

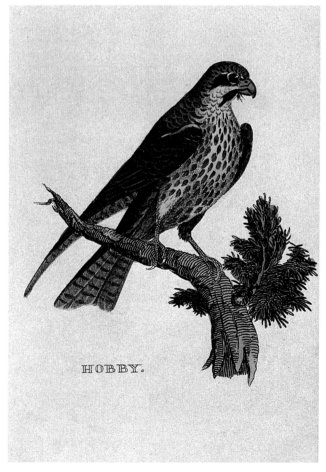

HOBBY.

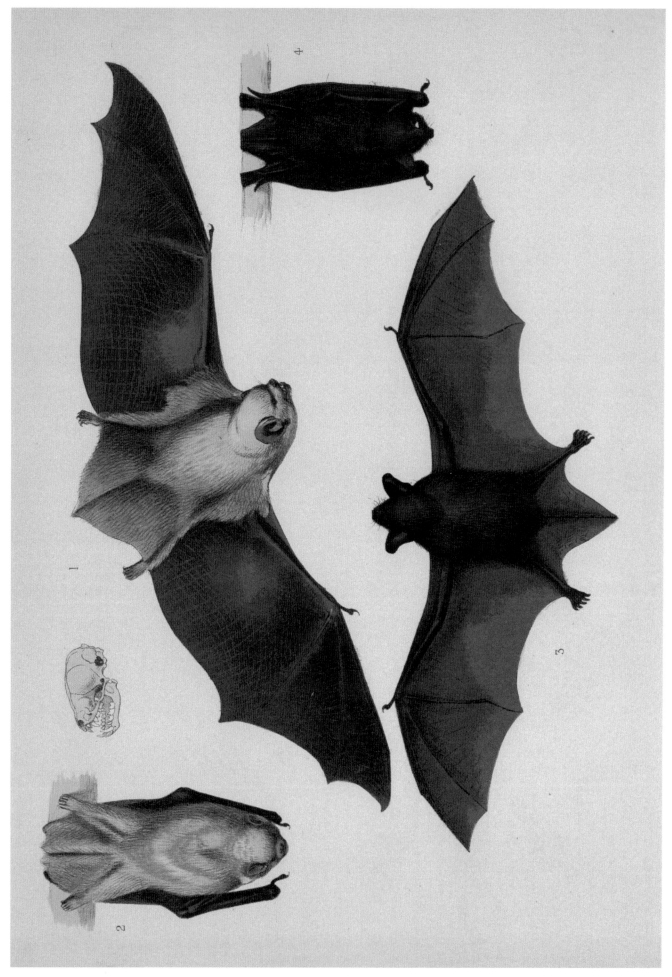

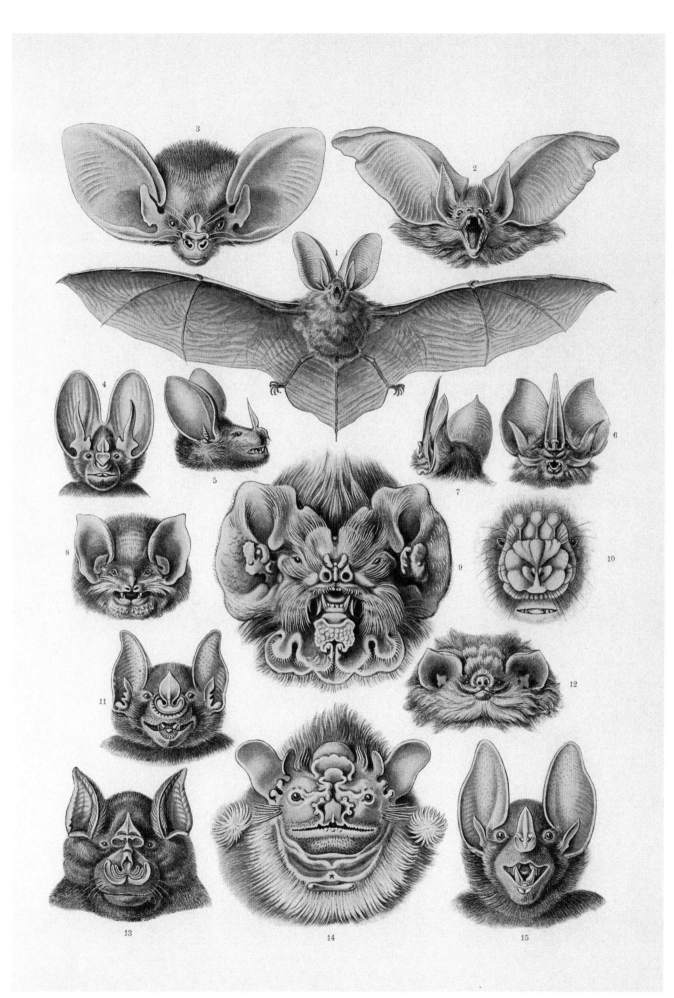

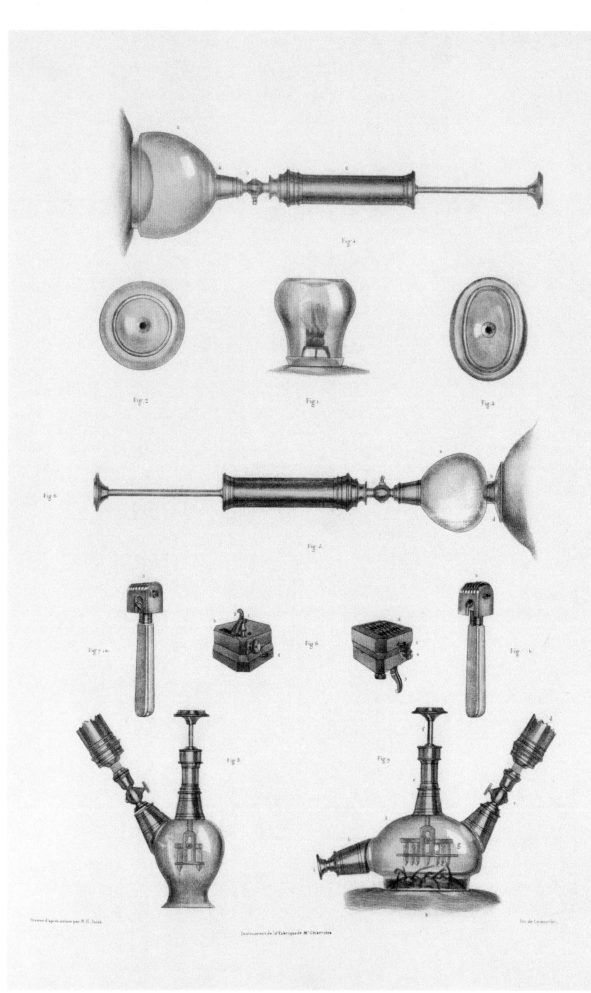

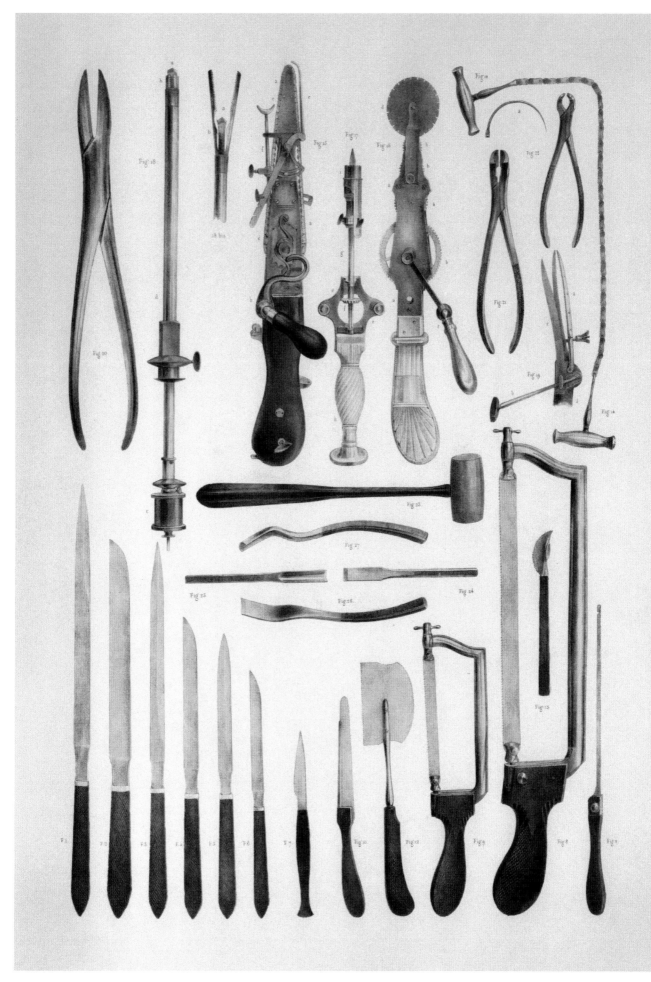

ELECTRICITY.

Plate I.

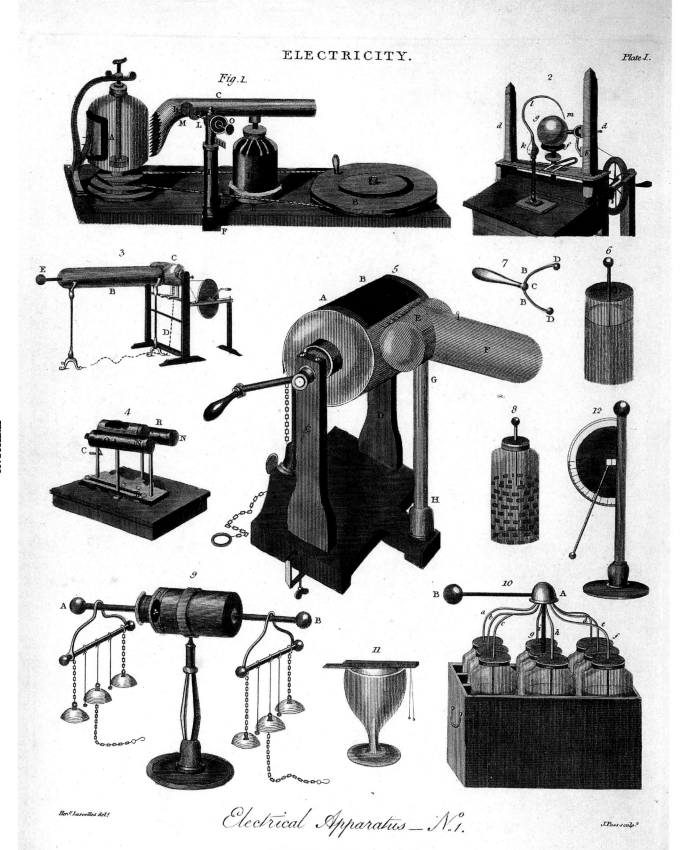

Fig. 1.

Electrical Apparatus _ Nᵒ. 1.

Henᵧ Lascelles delᵗ.

J.Pass sculpᵗ.

London Published as the Act directs Janᵧ 30 1804 by J.Wilkes.

CHEMISTRY.

Plate VIII.

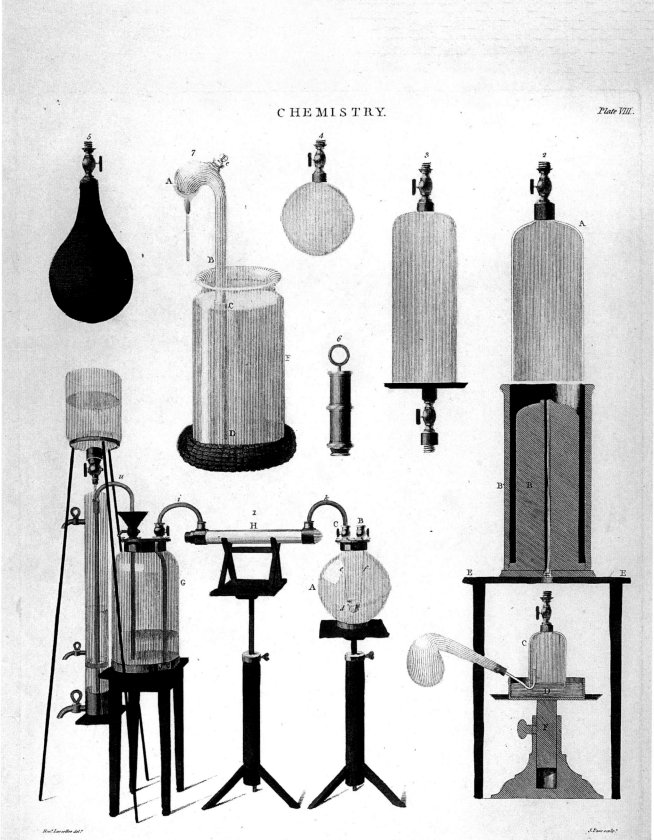

Hon.ᵉ Lascelles del.ᵗ

J.Pass sculp.ᵗ

1. Machine for the Combustion of Phosphorus. 2 to 6 The Mercurial Gazometer. 7 Guyton's Eudiometer.

London Published as the Act directs, Feb.ʸ 10.1803. by J.Wilkes.

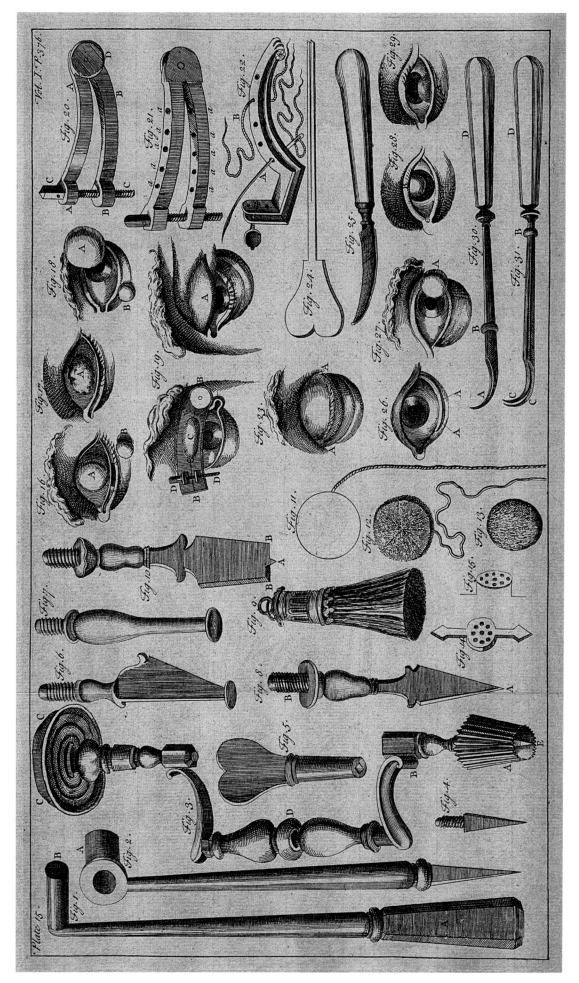

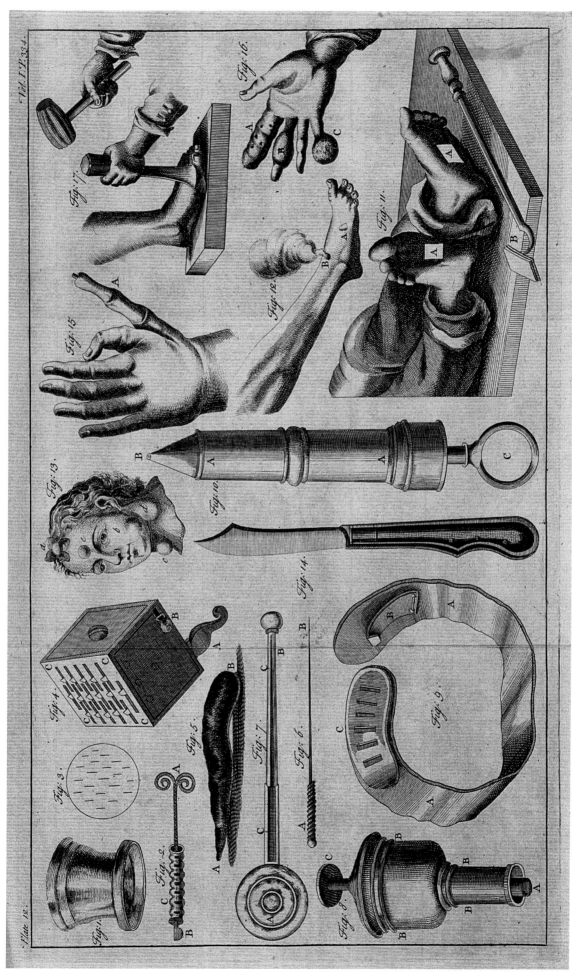

FARRIERY.

Plate III

Harquinier delt.

J. Pass sculp.

The principal layer of the Muscles after the fleshy Pannicle is removed.

London Published as the Act directs Nov.r 5.1805. by J.Wilkes.

FARRIERY.

Plate I.

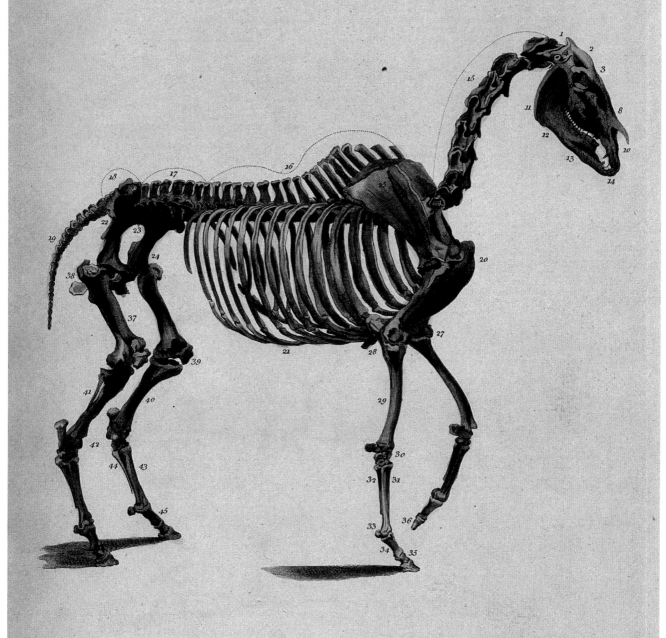

Skeleton, or Bones of the Horse.

London, Published as the Act directs, April 2, 1805, by J.Wilkes.

J.Pass sculp.

ANATOMY.

Plate III.

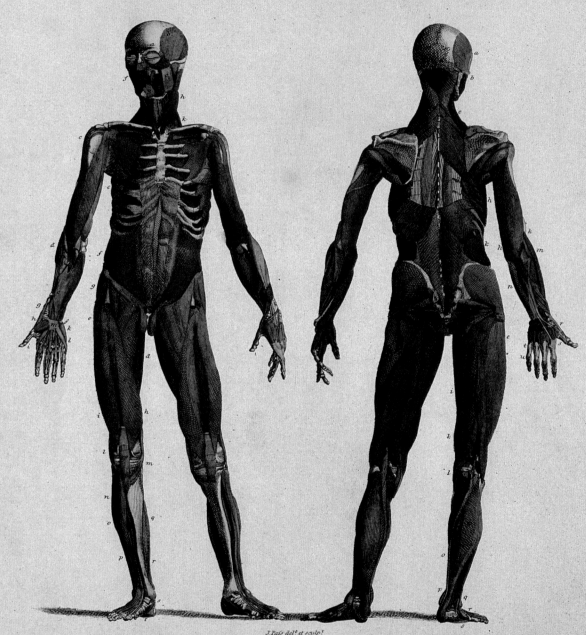

J. Pass del.t et sculp.t

A View of the second Layer of the Muscles.

London, Published as the Act directs, 9th April 1796, by J.Wilkes.

Plate I.

ANATOMY

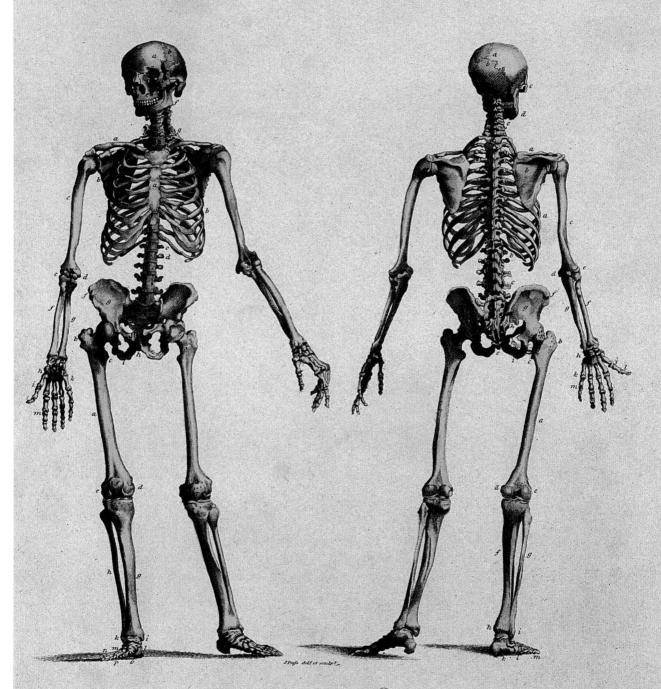

A front and back View of the Human Bones.

FARRIERY.

Plate X.

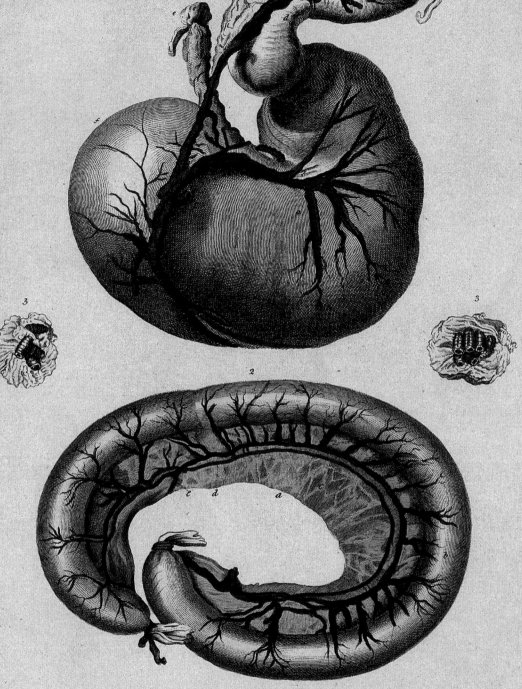

Harguinier del.

J.Pass sculp.

The Stomach, Mesentery, and Duodenum.

London. Published as the Act directs, April 13. 1805. by J.Wilkes.

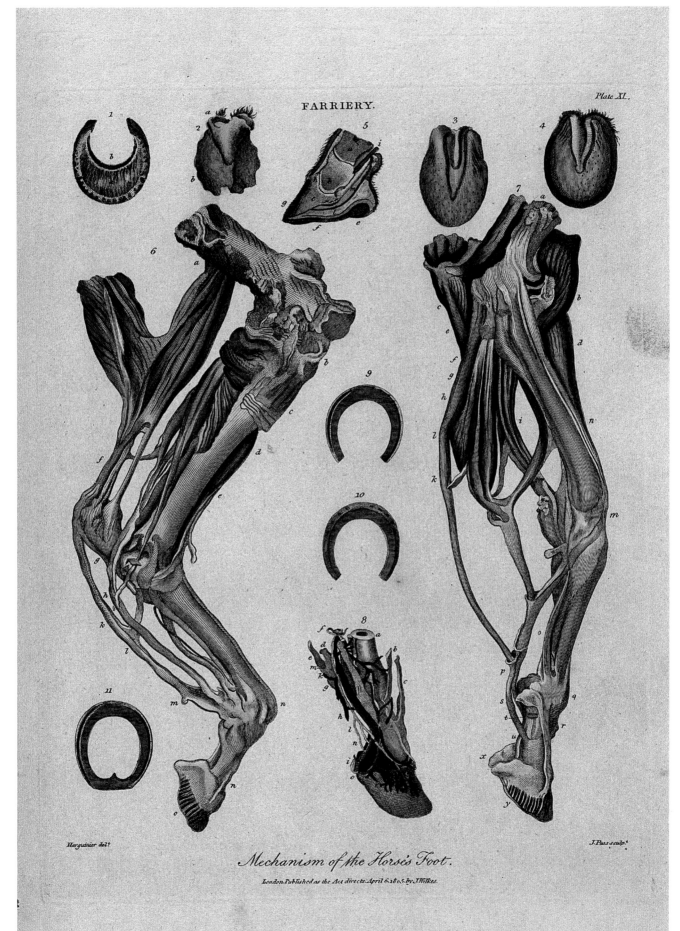

FARRIERY.

Plate XL.

Hargutnier delt

J.Pass sculp.

Mechanism of the Horse's Foot.

London.Published as the Act directs April 6.1805.by J.Wilkes.

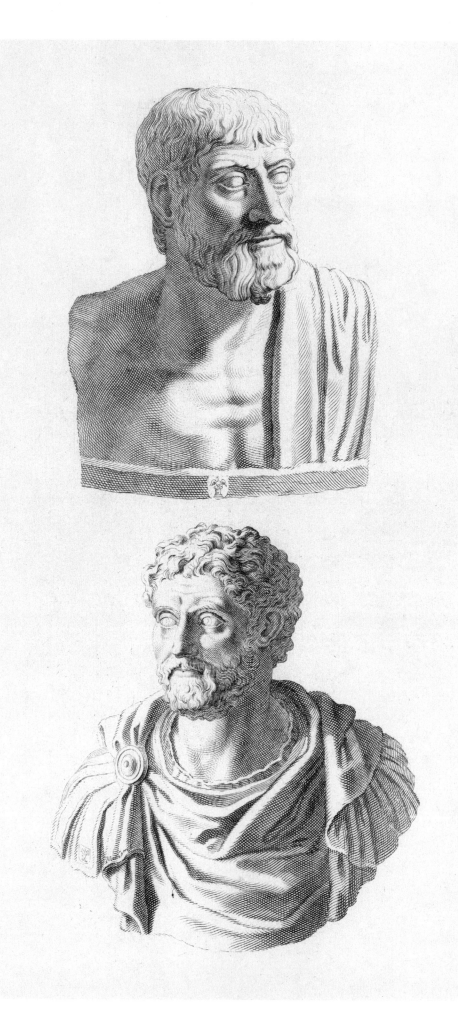

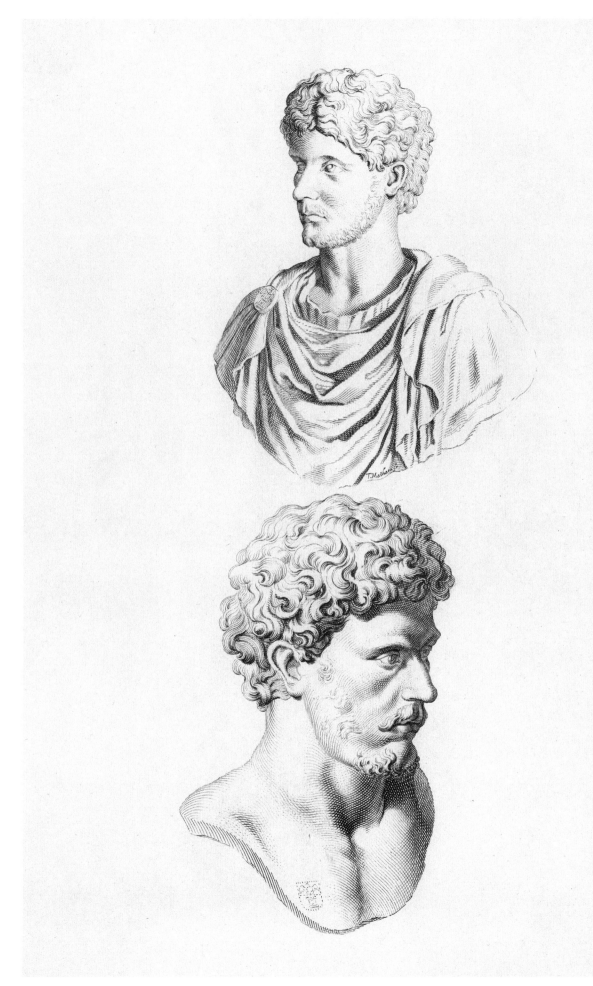

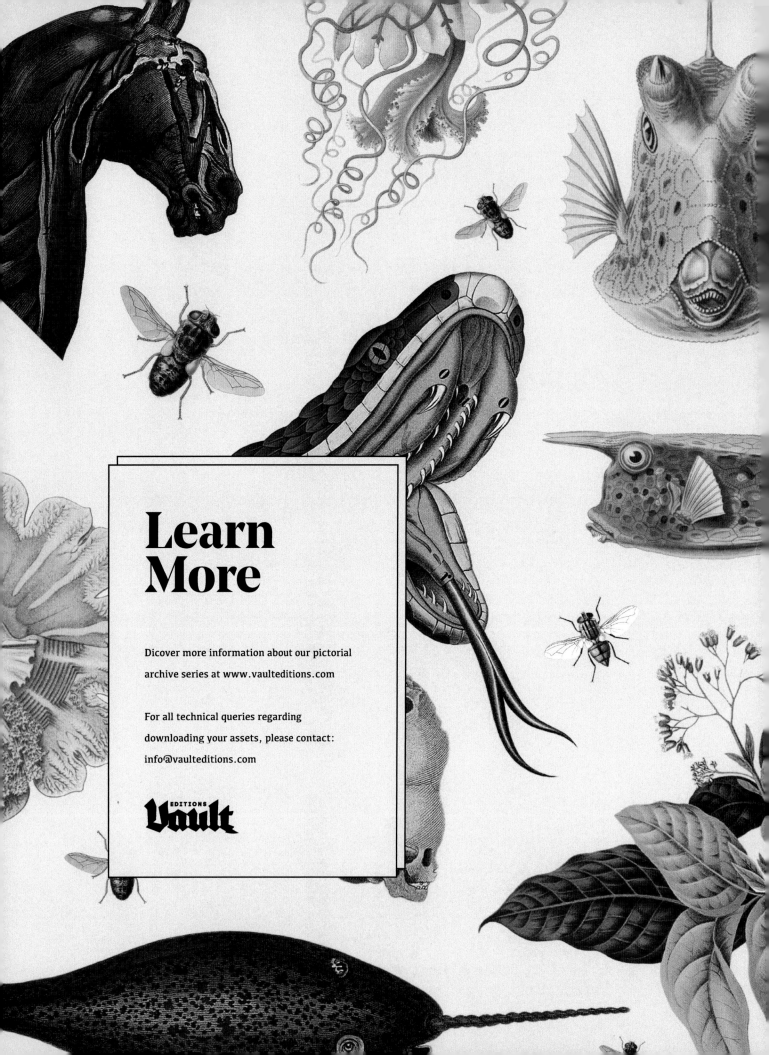

Learn
More

Dicover more information about our pictorial

archive series at www.vaulteditions.com

For all technical queries regarding

downloading your assets, please contact:

info@vaulteditions.com

EDITIONS
Vault